Overcoming Overthinking For Teenagers

Mindfulness Skills to Help Young Adults Manage Anxiety and Stress

Mary W. Bond

TABLE OF CONTENTS

Introduction

I remember the first time I was overwhelmed by my own thoughts. It felt like I was stuck in a maze, but instead of walls, there were endless questions, fears, and "what-ifs." My mind raced from one worry to the next, like a hamster on a wheel that just wouldn't stop. Even when I wanted to relax, even when I told myself I was fine—those anxious thoughts kept creeping in, weighing me down, pulling me into spirals I couldn't seem to escape.

If you've ever found yourself replaying the same scenario in your head, or you've struggled to quiet that persistent voice telling you something bad might happen, then you already know what it feels like to be trapped in overthinking. You tell yourself, "Just stop worrying," but it's like telling a river to stop flowing—it just doesn't work that way. And if you're a teenager, dealing with school, friends, family, and the pressure to figure out who you are in a world that demands so much of you, that mental noise can be deafening.

I know what you're going through, because I've been there myself. And that's why I wrote this book—because I wish someone had given me the tools to quiet my mind when I was younger. I wish someone had told me that it's possible to break free from the constant chatter in your head. But more than that, I want you to understand that you aren't alone. So many teens feel exactly like you do, facing the same struggles, the same fears, and the same feelings of being stuck.

This book is here to help you with something we all need to work on—overcoming overthinking.

It's a strange thing, isn't it? The way your mind can create its own storms, even when everything around you seems calm. Sometimes it feels like no one understands, like you're the only one dealing with this. You see your friends acting confident, smiling, and living their lives without a care, and you wonder, "What's wrong with me?" But here's the truth: even those who seem like they've got it all together are likely battling their own thoughts too. They just don't talk about it.

What you're feeling—the anxiety, the stress, the overthinking—it's not a flaw in you. It's a sign that your brain is working too hard to protect you, that it's getting stuck in overdrive trying to solve problems that haven't even happened yet. Your mind is doing what it thinks it should, but it doesn't have to be that way.

What if I told you there's a way to break free from this cycle?

Imagine waking up without immediately being flooded with a thousand worries about what might go wrong today. Imagine being able to focus on the things you care about—your friends, your hobbies, your goals—without your thoughts pulling you in every direction. Imagine having the tools to calm yourself when anxiety shows up and to take control of your thoughts before they take control of you.

This is possible, and you're closer to it than you think.

Through this book, we'll explore the power of mindfulness—a tool that has helped countless people of all ages manage their anxious minds. Mindfulness is about being present, fully in the moment, without letting your thoughts carry you away. It's about noticing your feelings without letting them control you. And while it may sound simple, the effects can be life-changing.

I want you to picture this: the next time you're caught in a loop of overthinking, instead of being overwhelmed, you'll have the skills to pause. You'll be able to step back, take a breath, and recognize your thoughts for what they are—just thoughts. You'll learn how to shift your focus away from those racing fears and into the present moment, where you are safe, where everything is okay, and where you have the power to choose your next step.

But this journey isn't about quick fixes. It's about building new habits, new ways of thinking, and learning how to be kind to yourself along the way. I'm not here to tell you that overthinking will disappear overnight. I'm here to tell you that with practice, patience, and the right tools, it gets easier. You'll begin to notice the quiet moments, the pauses between your thoughts, and in those moments, you'll find peace.

You'll also discover that managing anxiety and stress doesn't mean avoiding challenges or running away from discomfort. It means learning to face them with a calm and focused mind. It means understanding that you can't control everything that happens, but you can control how you respond. And that's where your true power lies.

In the chapters ahead, we'll break down what overthinking really is—why it happens, how it affects you, and most importantly, how to stop it from running your life. We'll talk about practical mindfulness exercises you can use every day, from grounding techniques to meditation, that will help you stay centered even when life feels chaotic. You'll learn how to recognize the triggers that send you into overthinking mode, and how to respond to them in a way that leaves you feeling empowered, not overwhelmed.

I've filled this book with stories, examples, and exercises that will guide you through this process step by step. You'll hear from other teens who've struggled with the same challenges, and you'll see how they've managed to turn things around. You'll get to try out different mindfulness techniques until you find the ones that work best for you, and by the end, you'll have a toolbox of skills you can rely on whenever life gets tough.

My hope is that as you read this book, you'll feel a sense of relief. Relief in knowing that you're not alone, and relief in knowing that you can do something about the stress and anxiety that overthinking brings. You're stronger than you realize, and with the right tools, you have everything you need to overcome this.

So, let's begin this journey together. Let's quiet the noise, calm the chaos, and take back control. Overthinking doesn't have to define you, and it certainly doesn't have to dictate your life. With mindfulness, you'll learn to navigate the challenges that come your way with clarity and confidence. It's time to break free from the cycle and discover what it feels like to live in the moment, fully present, without your mind running away with you.

Are you ready? Let's do this—one mindful step at a time.

Chapter 1: Understanding Overthinking and Anxiety

The Overthinking Trap: Why Teens Overthink

Overthinking is like a maze that seems easy to escape at first, but the deeper you go, the more complicated and disorienting it becomes. For teenagers, the mind is often an incredibly complex and dynamic place, brimming with thoughts, emotions, and perceptions that can easily spiral out of control. In fact, the teenage brain is particularly vulnerable to overthinking due to its developmental stage. Teens often find themselves trapped in loops of excessive thinking, ruminating over what they should have said, worrying about what others think of them, or obsessing over their future.

But what exactly drives teens to overthink, and why does it feel like their thoughts are working against them?

The Teenage Brain: A Work in Progress

First, it's crucial to understand that adolescence is a period of rapid brain development. During these years, the prefrontal cortex, which is responsible for decision-making, planning, and regulating emotions, is still under construction. Meanwhile, the limbic system—the part of the brain that processes emotions—develops much more quickly. This imbalance can lead to heightened emotions and impulsive reactions. In other words, teens often feel things more intensely, but their ability to manage these emotions is still catching up.

This developmental mismatch sets the stage for overthinking. When emotions run high, the brain tries to make sense of them, often leading to overanalysis. Without the fully mature prefrontal cortex to regulate these feelings, teens are more likely to get stuck in endless cycles of overthinking, searching for solutions to problems that may not even exist. This is one reason why simple situations, like a text message left unanswered, can evolve into a full-blown crisis in a teen's mind.

Perfectionism and Pressure: The Role of Expectations

Modern teenagers are under immense pressure—academically, socially, and personally. They're often expected to excel in school, maintain active social lives, participate in extracurricular activities, and plan for a future that feels uncertain. The pressure to be perfect or to meet impossible standards fuels overthinking.

Imagine this: a teen is preparing for a big exam. Instead of focusing on studying, they start worrying about what will happen if they fail. "What if I bomb the test? What if this ruins my GPA? What if I can't get into college?" These "what if" questions lead to a cascade of stressful thoughts. The more they think, the worse they feel, and the worse they feel, the more they continue to overthink. It's an exhausting mental loop, one that can leave teens feeling paralyzed by indecision and anxiety.

This kind of overthinking doesn't just apply to school. Social expectations are another huge driver. Teens live in a world saturated with social media, where their every action, appearance, and word can be scrutinized and compared. They might overanalyze every conversation they had that day, replaying it in their mind to find out if they said the "right" thing, if they were funny enough, cool enough, or liked enough. Did their friend really mean that compliment? Why didn't they get a "like" on that post? These seemingly trivial concerns can quickly escalate into self-doubt and emotional distress.

The Fear of Judgment and Social Comparison

Teens are particularly susceptible to overthinking when it comes to how they're perceived by others. Social comparison is deeply rooted in human psychology, but during adolescence, it becomes especially powerful. Teens are at a stage where their sense of identity is still forming, and as a result, they often look to their peers for validation. The problem is, this comparison frequently leads to feelings of inadequacy.

When teens overthink social situations, they're often doing so out of a fear of judgment. They might think, "What if they think I'm awkward?" or "What if they don't like me?" These questions can grow into a persistent worry, leading them to avoid certain social situations altogether. Ironically, the fear of being judged can become so overwhelming that it makes teens feel more isolated, even though they crave connection.

Social media amplifies this problem. The curated, filtered versions of life presented online create unrealistic standards that teens feel pressured to meet. They overthink their appearance, their social interactions, and their achievements, constantly comparing themselves to an ideal that doesn't actually exist. This endless comparison can make teens feel like they're never enough, which leads to more overthinking, creating a vicious cycle of self-criticism and anxiety.

Catastrophizing: Imagining the Worst Possible Outcomes

One of the most common cognitive patterns in overthinking is catastrophizing—imagining the worst-case scenario in every situation. For teens, this might look like spiraling from a small, everyday event to a major life catastrophe in a matter of minutes. For example, getting a poor grade on a test might lead to thoughts like, "I'll never get into college," or "This will ruin my entire future."

Catastrophizing is a defense mechanism the brain uses to try and protect itself. By imagining the worst, we think we're preparing for it. But in reality, this kind of thinking only increases anxiety and stress, causing teens to feel overwhelmed by problems that haven't even happened yet—and likely never will.

Over time, this negative thinking pattern can make teens feel hopeless and disempowered. The more they catastrophize, the less they trust in their ability to handle life's challenges. This is particularly harmful during adolescence, a time when young people are supposed to be building confidence in their ability to navigate the world. Instead, overthinking erodes that confidence, replacing it with doubt and fear.

Rumination: Stuck in the Past, Paralyzed by the Future
Another harmful aspect of overthinking is rumination, which involves obsessively dwelling on past events or mistakes. For teens, rumination might look like replaying an embarrassing moment over and over in their mind or fixating on a regretful decision. This mental habit can be particularly harmful because it traps them in a loop of negative thoughts, preventing them from moving forward.

While it's normal to reflect on the past, rumination takes it to an extreme, turning reflection into a source of anxiety. Instead of learning from past experiences and moving on, teens who ruminate are constantly replaying the same scenarios, often with a sense of self-criticism. They might think, "I should have done that differently," or "Why did I say that? They must think I'm so stupid." These thoughts are not only unproductive, but they also magnify the emotional pain of past mistakes, making it harder for teens to forgive themselves and grow.

In addition to being stuck in the past, overthinking can also paralyze teens with worry about the future. They may spend excessive time thinking about what might happen, imagining all the ways things could go wrong. This fear of the unknown can prevent them from taking action, as they get caught up in the "what ifs" rather than focusing on what they can control in the present.

Breaking Free from the Overthinking Trap
The good news is that overthinking, while common, is not inevitable. Teens can learn to manage and reduce their overthinking habits by developing greater self-awareness and practicing mindfulness techniques. It's important for teens to recognize when they're overthinking and to challenge the negative thoughts that are fueling their anxiety.

Mindfulness, which involves staying present and focused on the here and now, is one of the most effective tools for combating overthinking. When teens practice mindfulness, they learn to observe their thoughts without getting caught up in them. They can begin to differentiate between helpful problem-solving and unproductive rumination. By grounding themselves in the present moment, teens can break free from the endless loops of "what if" and "should have," allowing them to engage more fully in their lives without the constant burden of overanalysis.

In addition to mindfulness, it's essential for teens to develop self-compassion. Overthinking is often driven by a harsh inner critic, one that scrutinizes every mistake and imagines every possible failure. By learning to be kinder to themselves, teens can begin to quiet that critic, reducing the pressure they feel to be perfect.

Lastly, helping teens reframe their negative thoughts can be a powerful way to reduce overthinking. Instead of imagining the worst-case scenario, they can learn to challenge those thoughts with evidence. For example, if a teen is worried about a friend being mad at them, they can ask themselves, "What evidence do I have for that?" or "Is there another explanation for their behavior?" This kind of cognitive restructuring helps teens see situations more clearly, without the emotional distortion caused by overthinking.

Overthinking is a significant mental health challenge for teenagers, but it doesn't have to be a lifelong struggle. By understanding why they overthink and learning strategies to break free from this trap, teens can reclaim their mental clarity and emotional balance. With practice, they can move from a place of anxious rumination to one of mindful presence, where their thoughts no longer control them but instead serve as tools for growth and resilience.

What Happens in Your Brain During Anxiety

When you experience anxiety, it's not just a feeling or a fleeting thought. Anxiety is deeply rooted in the brain, engaging a complex network of neural circuits and processes. To understand anxiety from a neurobiological perspective, it's essential to break down how the brain's regions interact and why those interactions lead to the emotional and physical symptoms that characterize anxiety.

The Amygdala: Your Brain's Alarm System

At the core of your brain's anxiety response is the **amygdala**, a small, almond-shaped structure that acts as the brain's alarm system. The amygdala is crucial for processing emotions, particularly fear. When you encounter a potential threat—whether real or perceived—your amygdala springs into action. It alerts your brain and body that something might be dangerous, triggering a cascade of responses designed to protect you. This is why, when you're anxious, you might feel on edge, hyper-aware, or like you're in a state of heightened alertness.

The amygdala doesn't discriminate between physical threats, like a speeding car, and emotional ones, such as public speaking or social rejection. It reacts to anything that feels threatening, which is why anxiety can be triggered in situations that aren't actually dangerous. This overactivity of the amygdala is one of the hallmarks of anxiety disorders, causing you to feel like you're constantly in "fight-or-flight" mode even when there's no real danger.

The Hypothalamus and the Fight-or-Flight Response

Once the amygdala sounds the alarm, it sends a signal to the **hypothalamus**, which is the command center for your body's stress response. The hypothalamus activates the **sympathetic nervous system**, kicking off the fight-or-flight response. This is where things start to get physical.

In response, your **adrenal glands** release stress hormones like **adrenaline** and **cortisol**. These hormones flood your body, increasing your heart rate, elevating your blood pressure, and sharpening your senses. They prime your body to either fight the danger or flee from it. You might notice that your palms get sweaty, your muscles tense up, and your breathing becomes shallow and rapid. These physical sensations are all tied to the brain's efforts to prepare you for action, even if you're just sitting in a classroom worrying about an exam or lying in bed ruminating about your future.

The Prefrontal Cortex: The Voice of Reason

While the amygdala is responsible for emotional reactivity, the **prefrontal cortex (PFC)** is the brain's logical and rational control center. It helps you make sense of situations, evaluate risks, and make decisions. In theory, the PFC should balance out the amygdala's alarm system by telling you, "Hey, this isn't that big of a deal." However, when you're anxious, the connection between the prefrontal cortex and the amygdala can weaken, meaning your brain's rational voice gets drowned out by the emotional noise.

This is why, even though part of you knows that your fear is irrational—like being terrified of speaking up in a group or feeling overwhelming dread over a small mistake—you still feel consumed by anxiety. The amygdala is running the show, and the prefrontal cortex is struggling to regain control.

The Hippocampus: Memory and Anxiety

Another key player in anxiety is the **hippocampus**, which is responsible for storing and retrieving memories. This region helps contextualize your fears. For instance, if you've had a bad experience with public speaking in the past, your hippocampus will remind you of that event whenever you're in a similar situation, contributing to your anxiety.

The hippocampus can also be affected by chronic anxiety and stress. Studies show that prolonged exposure to high levels of stress hormones, like cortisol, can actually shrink the hippocampus. This makes it harder to process memories clearly and distinguish between past events and present situations, perpetuating the cycle of anxiety.

The Role of Neurotransmitters: Chemical Messengers

Your brain also relies on **neurotransmitters**—chemical messengers that transmit signals between neurons—to regulate mood and emotional responses. Three key neurotransmitters involved in anxiety are **serotonin**, **dopamine**, and **gamma-aminobutyric acid (GABA)**.

- **Serotonin** is often referred to as the "feel-good" neurotransmitter. It plays a critical role in regulating mood, and imbalances in serotonin levels are strongly linked to anxiety and depression. When serotonin levels are low, you might feel more prone to anxiety and less capable of managing stress.
- **Dopamine** is involved in motivation and reward processing. In the context of anxiety, dopamine imbalances can contribute to feelings of dread or impending doom, especially in situations where you feel you can't meet certain expectations or perform as desired.
- **GABA** is your brain's natural calming agent. It inhibits overexcitement and helps slow down neural activity when necessary. People with anxiety often have lower levels of GABA, which can make it difficult to "turn off" anxious thoughts and feelings, leading to chronic worry.

The HPA Axis: Your Stress Circuit

The **HPA (hypothalamic-pituitary-adrenal) axis** is a network of glands and hormones that regulate your body's stress response. When the amygdala signals a threat, the HPA axis jumps into action, coordinating the release of cortisol. This process is essential for short-term survival, but chronic activation of the HPA axis—due to ongoing anxiety—can lead to problems.

Over time, an overactive HPA axis can contribute to conditions like **chronic stress**, **insomnia**, and even physical ailments such as **heart disease** and **digestive issues**. Anxiety, by keeping your HPA axis in constant overdrive, can exhaust your body and leave you feeling physically and emotionally drained.

How Anxiety Becomes a Habit: Neural Pathways

Your brain is constantly rewiring itself based on your experiences—a concept known as **neuroplasticity**. When you repeatedly experience anxiety in certain situations, you strengthen the neural pathways associated with that anxiety. This is why anxiety can feel like a default response; your brain becomes wired to expect fear and worry, even in situations that don't warrant it.

For example, if you always feel anxious before tests, your brain learns to associate tests with fear. Over time, even thinking about a test can trigger anxiety, without the actual test needing to be present. These neural pathways become "habits," and breaking the cycle requires new experiences and responses to rewire the brain.

The Vicious Cycle of Anxiety: How It Feeds Itself

Once your brain gets stuck in an anxiety loop, it can feel impossible to escape. The more anxious you feel, the more reactive your amygdala becomes. And the more active your amygdala is, the harder it becomes for your prefrontal cortex to step in and calm things down. This creates a **vicious cycle** where anxious thoughts feed physical symptoms, and physical symptoms reinforce anxious thoughts.

For instance, let's say you're worried about giving a presentation. Your amygdala senses a threat and activates your fight-or-flight response, causing you to feel jittery, your heart to race, and your stomach to churn. These physical sensations only serve to increase your anxiety, confirming your brain's belief that the situation is indeed dangerous. As your anxiety builds, your mind starts racing with thoughts like, "What if I mess up?" or "Everyone will think I'm stupid," which only fuels the fire.

How to Calm an Anxious Brain

The good news is that your brain is also equipped with mechanisms to calm anxiety. Practices like **mindfulness**, **deep breathing**, and **meditation** activate the **parasympathetic nervous system**, which counters the fight-or-flight response and restores balance. Mindfulness can strengthen the connection between the prefrontal cortex and the amygdala, allowing you to regain control over your emotions and reduce the intensity of your anxiety.

By learning to recognize and interrupt anxious patterns in the brain, you can begin to reshape your neural pathways. Over time, this can reduce your sensitivity to triggers and help you develop healthier responses to stress.

In conclusion, anxiety is not just "in your head"—it's deeply embedded in your brain's structure and chemistry. Understanding how different parts of the brain contribute to anxiety can help you recognize why you feel the way you do and empower you to take steps toward calming your anxious mind. The brain is incredibly adaptable, and with the right tools and strategies, it's possible to change how you respond to anxiety and regain a sense of control over your thoughts and feelings.

Recognizing Triggers and Early Signs of Stress

As teenagers, you're navigating a complex and often overwhelming world. There are pressures from school, friendships, social media, and even family expectations. At this stage in your life, it's easy to feel anxious or stressed, but recognizing the triggers and early signs of stress is key to preventing it from spiraling out of control.

Stress often feels like an invisible weight that creeps in when you least expect it, but the truth is, it usually starts with small, subtle signals that we often ignore or don't recognize. When left unchecked, stress can grow into a more serious problem, contributing to anxiety, overthinking, and even physical symptoms like headaches, stomachaches, or insomnia. Learning to recognize stress triggers and its early signs can give you the upper hand, empowering you to manage your emotions before they take over.

What Exactly Are Triggers?

Triggers are external or internal events, situations, or even thoughts that can provoke an emotional response. For many, stress triggers are subtle, while for others, they are glaringly obvious. Triggers vary from person to person, which is why it's crucial to get to know what your specific stress triggers are.

Think of triggers as the spark that lights the fire. For example, a looming deadline for an assignment may not bother some students, but for others, it's the kindling for an anxiety fire. A trigger could be something as significant as a conflict with a close friend, or as seemingly minor as an offhand comment from a peer. The key is that triggers are personal — what stresses you out might not stress out someone else.

Here are a few common types of triggers for teenagers:

- **Academic Pressure:** Exams, assignments, college applications — school-related responsibilities can quickly become overwhelming.
- **Social Pressures:** Fitting in, maintaining friendships, or fear of missing out (FOMO) on social media can cause serious emotional strain.
- **Family Expectations:** High expectations from parents or caregivers can create pressure to achieve perfection or meet specific goals.
- **Personal Insecurities:** Comparing yourself to others, feeling uncertain about your abilities, or struggling with body image issues.
- **Uncertainty About the Future:** Worrying about your future career, finances, or life path can create anxiety about the unknown.

How to Recognize Your Triggers

Now that you know what triggers are, how can you identify your own? Pay close attention to the situations that precede feelings of anxiety or stress. Sometimes the trigger is obvious — like getting a bad grade or arguing with a friend. Other times, it may be more difficult to identify. For example, you might find that after spending a long time scrolling on social media, you feel anxious or inadequate without understanding exactly why.

Here's a helpful exercise: Keep a stress journal. For a week or two, jot down any moments where you feel particularly stressed or anxious. Write down the situation and what was happening before you felt that way. Over time, you'll start to notice patterns in what tends to set you off. These patterns will help you become more mindful of your triggers.

Internal vs. External Triggers

It's also important to understand that triggers can be both **external** (from outside events or situations) and **internal** (coming from your thoughts and emotions).

- **External triggers** are events happening around you, like an argument with a friend, pressure from school, or social media posts that make you feel inadequate.
- **Internal triggers** come from within. These are your own thoughts, feelings, or memories that provoke a stress response. For example, you might feel stressed because you're thinking about all the things you have to do, or you're worried about failing.

Internal triggers are often harder to recognize because they feel like part of our normal thought process. But by practicing mindfulness and paying attention to your thought patterns, you can start to identify when your own thoughts are contributing to stress.

The Early Signs of Stress

Stress doesn't usually hit you all at once — it builds gradually. And while it can show up differently for everyone, there are some common early warning signs to watch out for. Recognizing these signs early allows you to intervene before stress becomes overwhelming. Here's what to look for:

1. Physical Signs of Stress

Your body often gives you the first clues that something is off. When you're stressed, your body releases hormones like cortisol and adrenaline, which can cause a number of physical symptoms:

- **Tension in the Body:** Do your shoulders feel tight? Is your jaw clenched? Muscle tension, especially in the neck, shoulders, and back, is a common sign of stress.
- **Headaches or Migraines:** Stress can cause tension headaches, often felt as a dull ache or pressure around the forehead or back of the head.

- **Stomach Issues:** Butterflies, nausea, or an upset stomach are all common physical responses to stress.
- **Changes in Sleep Patterns:** Struggling to fall asleep, waking up frequently, or sleeping more than usual can all signal stress.
- **Increased Heart Rate or Sweating:** Stress triggers your fight-or-flight response, which can make your heart race or cause sweating, even in non-threatening situations.

2. Emotional Signs of Stress

Emotionally, stress can make you feel on edge, overwhelmed, or anxious. These emotional signs can be tricky because they might feel like they're just part of your normal emotional landscape — but if they persist, they might be an early sign of stress:

- **Irritability or Mood Swings:** You might find yourself snapping at others or feeling annoyed by small things.
- **Feeling Overwhelmed:** You may feel like you're drowning in your responsibilities, with no way to keep up.
- **Anxiety or Worry:** Persistent worrying, especially about things outside your control, can be a sign that stress is building up.
- **Low Motivation:** Stress can zap your energy, making it hard to stay motivated, even with things you usually enjoy.
- **Feeling Down or Hopeless:** While not necessarily the same as depression, stress can lead to feelings of sadness, pessimism, or hopelessness.

3. Behavioral Signs of Stress

Stress also affects the way you behave. You might notice changes in your habits or the way you interact with others:

- **Avoidance:** Stress can cause you to avoid situations or people that trigger your anxiety. For example, you might start skipping school, avoiding friends, or procrastinating on tasks.
- **Withdrawal from Social Activities:** You might start pulling away from people or activities you usually enjoy because you feel too drained or overwhelmed.
- **Unhealthy Coping Mechanisms:** Some people turn to unhealthy habits when stressed, such as overeating, not eating enough, sleeping too much, or spending excessive time on their phones.
- **Difficulty Concentrating:** When your mind is preoccupied with stress, it's hard to focus on tasks. You might find that you're more forgetful or have trouble concentrating on schoolwork.

What Can You Do When You Recognize the Signs?

Recognizing stress early is crucial, but what's even more important is how you respond to it. When you start to notice the early signs of stress, here are some things you can do:

1. **Take a Break:** When stress starts to build, give yourself permission to step away. Even a short break can help reset your mind and body.
2. **Breathe:** Practice deep, mindful breathing. Inhale deeply for four counts, hold for four, and exhale for four. This helps activate your parasympathetic nervous system, which calms your stress response.
3. **Get Moving:** Physical activity is a powerful stress reliever. Go for a walk, dance around your room, or do some yoga to help release tension.
4. **Talk to Someone:** Sometimes just talking about what's stressing you out can help you feel better. Reach out to a friend, family member, or therapist if you need support.
5. **Practice Mindfulness:** Stay present and practice mindfulness techniques like meditation, grounding exercises, or simply being aware of your surroundings.
6. **Write It Out:** Journaling about your stress can help you process your feelings and get a better sense of what's going on in your mind.

Understanding your stress triggers and recognizing the early signs of stress is like gaining a superpower. It allows you to take control of your mental and emotional health before stress becomes overwhelming. By becoming more aware of your body, emotions, and behaviors, you can build resilience and prevent stress from negatively impacting your life. Remember, stress is a normal part of life, but how you handle it makes all the difference.

Chapter 2: Breaking the Cycle of Anxiety

How Anxiety Feeds Itself

Anxiety, by nature, is a deeply ingrained survival mechanism that's evolved over centuries to protect us from threats. However, in today's world, many of the perceived threats aren't life-threatening but rather psychological—fears about social judgment, academic failure, or future uncertainty. When left unchecked, anxiety can spiral and feed into itself, creating a self-perpetuating loop that can be difficult to break. Understanding how anxiety works and the mechanisms by which it maintains its grip is crucial to managing it effectively.

The Evolution of Anxiety: From Survival to Psychological Stress

To begin, it's important to understand that anxiety isn't inherently harmful. In fact, it's part of the body's natural "fight or flight" response, designed to help us act quickly in dangerous situations. In the past, this meant fleeing from predators or reacting to immediate physical threats. The problem arises when this same response system is activated by everyday situations like exams, public speaking, or social interactions. These aren't physical dangers, but the brain treats them with the same urgency.

When we feel anxious, the amygdala (the brain's fear center) gets activated, signaling the body to release stress hormones like cortisol and adrenaline. These hormones increase heart rate, tighten muscles, and sharpen focus, preparing the body for action. However, unlike physical threats, modern stressors like overthinking, worrying about the future, or fearing judgment from peers don't require immediate action. They linger, triggering the same physiological responses over and over again. This constant state of alertness becomes exhausting, and over time, anxiety can begin to feed on itself.

The Cognitive Feedback Loop: How Thoughts Spiral

At the core of anxiety's self-perpetuation is a cognitive feedback loop—a vicious cycle where anxious thoughts lead to physical sensations of anxiety, which then reinforce the anxious thoughts. Here's a more detailed look at how this plays out:

1. **The Initial Thought:** Anxiety often begins with a "what if" thought—what if I fail this test? What if people judge me? These thoughts may seem harmless at first, but they can trigger the body's stress response. This thought doesn't have to be based on reality; it's the brain's way of preparing for any potential threat, no matter how unlikely.
2. **The Physical Response:** In response to this anxious thought, the body reacts as if the threat were real. You might feel your heart race, your palms get sweaty, or your stomach

churn. These sensations are uncomfortable and can make the original worry feel more valid. After all, if your body is reacting like this, something must be wrong, right?

3. **The Emotional Amplification:** Now that the body is in a state of heightened alert, the brain becomes even more focused on the perceived threat. You start to dwell on it, replaying the initial fear and imagining worst-case scenarios. The more you think about it, the more real it feels. Anxiety thrives on worst-case thinking, feeding off your attention and growing in intensity.

4. **The Negative Reinforcement:** The brain then begins to associate certain situations, thoughts, or even physical sensations with danger. For example, if public speaking makes you anxious, you might start to avoid it altogether. This avoidance, while relieving in the short term, only reinforces the idea that the situation is truly dangerous. The brain learns that avoiding these situations keeps you "safe," making it more likely to trigger anxiety the next time you face something similar.

The Role of Avoidance in the Cycle

Avoidance is a major factor in how anxiety feeds itself. When we feel anxious about something, whether it's speaking in front of others, facing a difficult conversation, or dealing with uncertainty, the natural impulse is to avoid it. This is a survival tactic—the brain wants to steer clear of discomfort or perceived danger. However, avoidance actually strengthens the anxiety in the long term.

Here's why: When you avoid something that causes you anxiety, you reinforce the idea that the situation is dangerous. Even if you know logically that the threat isn't real, your brain interprets avoidance as a survival strategy, reinforcing the idea that this situation is unsafe. Over time, the anxiety grows because your brain becomes conditioned to associate that situation with fear and danger.

For instance, if you're anxious about social situations, you might start to withdraw from social gatherings, meetings, or even casual interactions with friends. Initially, avoiding these situations may feel like a relief. But over time, the fear grows larger because you haven't allowed yourself to face and challenge it. This avoidance perpetuates the anxiety, making it feel even more daunting the next time the situation arises.

Catastrophizing and Cognitive Distortions

Another way anxiety feeds itself is through **cognitive distortions**, particularly a thinking pattern called *catastrophizing*. Catastrophizing is when you take a small, manageable worry and mentally blow it out of proportion, imagining the worst possible outcome. For example, if you're worried about an upcoming exam, you might start to think, "What if I fail? If I fail, I'll never get into college. If I don't get into college, my entire future is ruined." This chain of thoughts takes a relatively small stressor and turns it into a full-blown crisis in your mind.

This type of thinking fuels anxiety because it triggers the brain's fear response for something that hasn't happened and may never happen. The brain doesn't differentiate between imagined fears and real threats, so every time you engage in catastrophic thinking, your body reacts as if it's facing an immediate danger. This creates a cycle where anxiety breeds more anxiety, keeping you trapped in a loop of overthinking and fear.

Hypervigilance: The Over-Awareness of Threats

When you experience anxiety regularly, the brain starts to become **hypervigilant**, constantly scanning the environment for potential threats. Hypervigilance is another survival mechanism that becomes maladaptive in modern life. When your brain is in a constant state of alertness, you start to notice every small change in your environment or body and interpret it as a potential problem.

For example, a minor headache might be interpreted as a sign of something serious, or a neutral facial expression from a friend might be seen as disapproval. This hyperawareness can lead to more anxiety, as the brain finds "evidence" for its worries everywhere it looks. The more you focus on these perceived threats, the more anxious you feel, and the more your brain becomes convinced that there are constant dangers.

The Role of Rumination in Anxiety

Another way anxiety feeds itself is through **rumination**—the habit of continually thinking about and analyzing your worries. While it might seem productive to think about your problems, rumination often leads to overthinking and keeps you stuck in a cycle of fear. Instead of finding solutions, your brain replays the same worries over and over, magnifying the sense of threat.

Rumination can be especially damaging because it feels like you're addressing your worries, but in reality, you're only deepening your anxiety. The more you ruminate, the harder it becomes to break the cycle because your brain becomes accustomed to the constant mental activity around your fears. This mental churn creates a never-ending feedback loop that drains your mental energy and heightens your anxiety.

Breaking the Cycle of Anxiety

Breaking this cycle is challenging but possible. One of the most effective strategies is **mindfulness**—the practice of staying present in the moment and observing your thoughts without judgment. Mindfulness helps you break free from the anxious feedback loop by allowing you to see your thoughts as just thoughts, not facts. Instead of getting caught up in the "what if" spiral, you can learn to observe your anxiety with curiosity and compassion.

Cognitive Behavioral Therapy (CBT) is another powerful tool for breaking the cycle. CBT helps you identify and challenge cognitive distortions like catastrophizing and teaches you to reframe your thoughts in a more balanced and realistic way. By addressing these thought patterns, you can interrupt the feedback loop and reduce the intensity of your anxiety.

Finally, **exposure** to feared situations can help rewire the brain's anxiety response. By gradually facing the situations you've been avoiding, you can teach your brain that these situations aren't as dangerous as they seem. This process helps diminish the power of avoidance and breaks the reinforcement that anxiety needs to thrive.

Anxiety feeds itself through a combination of cognitive distortions, avoidance, hypervigilance, and rumination. These mechanisms keep the body in a constant state of alert, reinforcing the brain's belief that there are threats all around. Breaking this cycle requires a combination of mindfulness, cognitive restructuring, and gradual exposure to feared situations. With practice, it's possible to regain control over anxiety and live a life that isn't dominated by fear.

The Link Between Overthinking and Stress

In today's fast-paced, hyper-connected world, it's common for teens to feel overwhelmed. Schoolwork, social pressure, family expectations, and the constant buzz of social media all collide to create an environment where it's easy to overthink everything. But how exactly does overthinking tie into stress? To answer that, we need to dig deeper into the mental and emotional processes behind overthinking, how it impacts your body, and the strategies we can use to break the vicious cycle.

What Is Overthinking?

At its core, overthinking is the habit of getting stuck in a loop of repetitive thoughts. You might ruminate on a past mistake, worry about a future event, or analyze every single interaction you had during the day. It's like your brain is a broken record, playing the same track over and over without giving you relief or closure.

It's important to distinguish between **productive thinking**—the kind that helps you solve problems—and **overthinking**, which feels endless, consuming, and draining. While productive thinking leads to solutions and action, overthinking keeps you stuck. You analyze, you worry, but you don't actually get closer to making decisions or feeling better. And this constant mental loop can lead to or exacerbate stress, trapping you in a cycle that's hard to break.

Why Do We Overthink?

Overthinking often stems from anxiety and the brain's desire to control outcomes. When we're anxious, our mind enters a state of hypervigilance, trying to anticipate every possible scenario.

The brain believes that by thinking more, by anticipating every problem, it can prevent bad outcomes. But in reality, this overdrive doesn't result in control; it results in **mental exhaustion**.

For teens, this can be particularly intense. Navigating a world filled with academic pressure, friendship dynamics, social media, and parental expectations is no easy task. The teenage brain is still developing, especially the prefrontal cortex, which is responsible for decision-making and impulse control. This means the natural tendency to worry or obsess over details is amplified during adolescence. Add to that fluctuating hormones, peer comparison, and the pressure to fit in, and it's no wonder overthinking becomes a dominant habit.

How Overthinking Leads to Stress

When you overthink, your brain is constantly in "fight or flight" mode. This is a survival mechanism deeply rooted in our evolution. In prehistoric times, this response helped our ancestors deal with immediate threats, like a predator. However, modern-day stressors are more psychological than physical, yet they trigger the same biological response.

When you're stuck in an overthinking loop, your brain perceives your thoughts as threats. You replay a conversation you had earlier, wondering if you said something wrong, or you imagine how a situation might go wrong in the future. This causes your brain to release **cortisol**, the stress hormone, as if you're in danger. The problem is, you can't fight or flee from your own thoughts, so the stress response stays active, creating a heightened sense of tension that doesn't dissipate.

The Physical Toll of Overthinking-Induced Stress

The stress caused by overthinking isn't just mental—it manifests physically too. Chronic stress due to overthinking can lead to:

- **Tension headaches and migraines**: Your brain is working overtime, causing your muscles to tense up, particularly in your neck and shoulders.
- **Sleep disturbances**: The never-ending cycle of thoughts makes it hard to shut down at night, leading to insomnia or restless sleep.
- **Digestive issues**: Stress has a direct impact on the gut, potentially leading to stomachaches, nausea, or irritable bowel syndrome (IBS).
- **Weakened immune system**: Prolonged stress reduces your immune response, making you more vulnerable to illness.
- **Fatigue**: The constant mental processing drains your energy, leaving you physically and mentally exhausted.

Emotional and Behavioral Impact

Overthinking doesn't just affect your body—it can drastically change your emotional state and behavior. When you're trapped in this cycle, you might experience:

- **Increased anxiety**: Overthinking fuels anxiety, creating a feedback loop. The more you think about a problem, the more anxious you become, which then leads to more overthinking.
- **Irritability**: Small issues that wouldn't normally bother you can become overwhelming. You're on edge, more sensitive to criticism or conflict.
- **Procrastination**: Because overthinking makes every decision feel monumental, it can lead to avoidance. You might put off assignments or difficult conversations because you fear making the "wrong" choice.
- **Perfectionism**: You may become overly focused on making everything perfect, which adds more pressure and anxiety to your daily life.
- **Withdrawal from social situations**: You might start avoiding social interactions because you're constantly worried about saying or doing the wrong thing, or because you're exhausted from the mental strain.

The Cycle of Overthinking and Stress

Overthinking and stress create a self-reinforcing loop. Overthinking leads to stress, and stress makes you more prone to overthinking. Here's how it typically plays out:

1. **Trigger**: A stressor—whether it's a big exam, an argument with a friend, or an upcoming social event—activates your anxiety.
2. **Thought Spiral**: You start to overanalyze the situation, questioning every detail, wondering what could go wrong. This amplifies your anxiety.
3. **Stress Response**: Your brain perceives your worries as threats, triggering the fight-or-flight response. Your body is flooded with stress hormones like cortisol.
4. **Physical and Emotional Symptoms**: You start to feel the effects—headaches, restlessness, fatigue, irritability. These symptoms make you feel even more overwhelmed.
5. **More Overthinking**: Because you're physically and emotionally uncomfortable, you start overthinking more—trying to "fix" the problem in your mind. And the cycle continues.

Breaking the Overthinking-Stress Cycle

The good news is that while the overthinking-stress cycle is powerful, it's not unbreakable. Here are some strategies to help you interrupt this cycle:

1. Practice Mindfulness

Mindfulness is one of the most effective tools for breaking the cycle of overthinking. It teaches you to focus on the present moment, reducing the mental noise that overthinking creates. By bringing your attention back to your breath, your body, or your surroundings, you can quiet your mind and create space between you and your thoughts. The more you practice mindfulness, the easier it becomes to recognize when you're falling into an overthinking spiral and bring yourself back to the present.

2. Challenge Your Thoughts

Not every thought deserves your attention. When you catch yourself overthinking, take a moment to ask: "Is this thought helpful? Is this based on fact or assumption?" By challenging your thoughts, you can begin to distinguish between helpful problem-solving and harmful rumination. Cognitive Behavioral Therapy (CBT) techniques can help you reframe negative thoughts and replace them with more balanced, realistic ones.

3. Take Action, Even if It's Imperfect

One of the most effective ways to stop overthinking is to take action, even if you're uncertain or scared. Overthinking often paralyzes you, making every decision feel overwhelming. But when you take a small step, even if it's imperfect, it breaks the cycle of inaction. This sends a signal to your brain that you're not helpless, and that can significantly reduce stress.

4. Create Boundaries for Your Thoughts

If you're prone to overthinking, set boundaries. You can designate a specific time of day, say 15 minutes, to think about your worries or challenges. Outside of that time, give yourself permission to let those thoughts go. You can even write down your concerns to "release" them, so they're not swirling around in your head all day.

5. Incorporate Relaxation Techniques

Since overthinking triggers the body's stress response, relaxation techniques can help soothe your nervous system and bring you out of fight-or-flight mode. Deep breathing exercises, progressive muscle relaxation, and guided imagery can calm your body and, in turn, quiet your mind.

The link between overthinking and stress is strong, but it's not unbreakable. Understanding how they feed into each other is the first step toward freeing yourself from the mental and physical toll they take. By practicing mindfulness, challenging negative thoughts, taking small actions, and setting boundaries for your mental energy, you can regain control over your thoughts and reduce the stress that overthinking causes.

It won't happen overnight. Overthinking can feel like an ingrained habit, and it may take time to rewire your brain's default mode. But with patience, self-compassion, and consistent practice, you can break the cycle and find relief from the overwhelming pressure of overthinking. The key is to remember that your thoughts are just that—thoughts. They don't define you, and they don't have to control your life.

Shifting from Worry to Action

Worry can feel like an endless cycle, a repetitive loop of thoughts that drains our energy and clouds our judgment. For many teenagers, this cycle becomes a barrier to taking action and achieving their goals. But shifting from worry to action is not only possible; it's essential for mental well-being and personal growth. In this chapter, we'll explore the nature of worry, the reasons we often get stuck in this cycle, and, most importantly, practical steps to empower you to break free and take action.

Understanding Worry

Worry is a natural response to uncertainty. It's your mind's way of trying to prepare for the unknown or protect you from potential threats. While a small amount of worry can be helpful—prompting you to study for an exam or think ahead about future plans—excessive worry can become paralyzing. It often manifests as:

- **Ruminating**: Replaying past events in your mind, questioning what you could have done differently.
- **Catastrophizing**: Imagining the worst possible outcomes, even when the likelihood of those outcomes is low.
- **Avoidance**: Delaying decisions or actions because you're afraid of making the wrong choice.

These patterns can create a mental fog, making it difficult to see clear paths forward. The mind, in its attempt to protect you, may inadvertently trap you in a cycle of inaction.

The Impact of Worry on Your Life

Excessive worry can affect various aspects of your life, including your:

- **Emotional Health**: Constant worrying can lead to anxiety, depression, and feelings of helplessness. When your mind is consumed with worry, it can overshadow positive thoughts and experiences.

- **Physical Health**: Chronic worry can manifest in physical symptoms like headaches, stomachaches, fatigue, and sleep disturbances. Your body responds to stress and worry as if it's under threat, which can lead to a cascade of health issues.
- **Social Life**: Worry can isolate you from friends and family. You might avoid social situations because you're afraid of being judged or embarrassed, leading to loneliness and missed connections.
- **Academic and Career Goals**: When worry prevents you from acting, it can stifle your academic performance and career aspirations. Procrastination often follows worry, resulting in missed deadlines and opportunities.

Why We Struggle to Shift from Worry to Action

1. **Fear of Failure**: The prospect of failure can be daunting. When you're worried about making the wrong choice, it can feel safer to do nothing rather than risk a perceived failure.
2. **Perfectionism**: Many teenagers hold themselves to impossibly high standards. The belief that you must do something perfectly can lead to paralyzing self-doubt and inaction.
3. **Lack of Confidence**: If you struggle with self-esteem, taking action can feel overwhelming. Worrying about your abilities may prevent you from pursuing your goals.
4. **Overthinking**: Analyzing every detail can be counterproductive. While it's important to consider your options, overthinking can lead to indecision and procrastination.
5. **Social Pressure**: Peer expectations can amplify worry. You may fear how your actions will be perceived by others, leading to hesitation and self-doubt.

Steps to Shift from Worry to Action

1. **Recognize Your Worry**: The first step in shifting from worry to action is to acknowledge your feelings. Journaling can be a powerful tool here. Write down what you're worried about, how it makes you feel, and any specific thoughts that keep circling in your mind. This process can help externalize your worries and make them feel more manageable.
2. **Challenge Negative Thoughts**: After identifying your worries, ask yourself if they are rational. Are you catastrophizing? Are you stuck in a loop of negative thinking? Challenge these thoughts by asking yourself:
   - What evidence do I have that this worry will come true?
   - What would I tell a friend who was experiencing this worry?
   - Have I been in a similar situation before, and how did it turn out?
3. **Set Small, Achievable Goals**: Breaking your tasks into smaller, manageable steps can alleviate the overwhelm. Instead of thinking, "I have to ace this exam," break it down to "I will study for 30 minutes today." Celebrate each small victory, as this can boost your confidence and motivation.

4. **Practice Mindfulness**: Mindfulness techniques can help ground you in the present moment, reducing the intensity of your worries. Simple practices like deep breathing, meditation, or mindful walking can provide clarity and calm your racing thoughts.

5. **Create an Action Plan**: Once you've identified a worry, turn it into a plan of action. Ask yourself:
   - What is the first step I can take to address this worry?
   - Who can I talk to for support or guidance?
   - What resources are available to help me move forward?

6. **Embrace Imperfection**: Understand that not every action you take needs to be perfect. Embrace the idea that mistakes are part of growth. Reflect on past experiences where you learned valuable lessons from your missteps.

7. **Visualize Success**: Visualization can be a powerful tool for shifting from worry to action. Spend a few minutes each day picturing yourself successfully navigating the situation you're worried about. Imagine the steps you take, the emotions you feel, and the positive outcome. This technique can help increase your confidence and reduce anxiety.

8. **Limit Exposure to Triggers**: Identify situations or environments that amplify your worry and try to limit your exposure to them. If social media causes you to compare yourself negatively to others, consider taking a break. Protecting your mental space can help you focus more on taking actionable steps.

9. **Seek Support**: Sometimes, sharing your worries with someone you trust can alleviate their weight. Whether it's a friend, family member, or therapist, talking through your feelings can provide perspective and support. They can help you brainstorm solutions or simply listen without judgment.

10. **Take Action**: Ultimately, the best way to break the cycle of worry is to take action, even if it's a small one. Start by doing something related to your worry that feels manageable. This could mean studying a little for that exam, reaching out to a friend, or applying for a job. Action breeds confidence, and the momentum can help propel you forward.

Embracing a New Mindset

Shifting from worry to action isn't about eliminating worry entirely; it's about learning to navigate it effectively. As you practice these techniques, you'll develop a new mindset—one that acknowledges worry but doesn't allow it to dictate your choices. Remember, every small step counts. The journey from worry to action is a process, and it's okay to move at your own pace.

By taking control of your thoughts and actions, you can reclaim your power. Embrace the possibilities that come with taking action, and watch as your worries transform into opportunities for growth and success. You are capable of more than you realize, and each step you take can lead you toward a brighter, more empowered future.

Chapter 3: Mindfulness 101: Techniques to Stay Present

What Is Mindfulness?

Mindfulness is a mental practice that encourages individuals to focus on the present moment without judgment. At its core, mindfulness is about awareness—awareness of thoughts, feelings, bodily sensations, and the surrounding environment. This practice has its roots in ancient meditation traditions, particularly within Buddhism, but in recent decades, it has gained widespread popularity in Western psychology as a valuable tool for managing stress, anxiety, and a host of other mental health challenges.

The Essence of Mindfulness

Imagine standing on the edge of a peaceful lake, watching as the ripples gently spread across the surface. In that moment, nothing else matters—there's no worry about tomorrow's homework, no regret about yesterday's mistakes, and no judgment about your feelings. This state of being, where you are fully immersed in the present moment, captures the essence of mindfulness.

Mindfulness invites you to step back from the constant stream of thoughts that often dominate our minds. It teaches us to observe our thoughts and feelings as they arise, rather than becoming entangled in them. Instead of reacting impulsively or getting swept away by anxiety, mindfulness empowers us to respond thoughtfully and deliberately.

The Science Behind Mindfulness

Research has shown that mindfulness has profound effects on both the brain and body. Studies using neuroimaging techniques have found that regular mindfulness practice can alter brain structures and functions, particularly in areas associated with attention, emotion regulation, and self-awareness. For instance, the prefrontal cortex—responsible for decision-making and impulse control—tends to be more active in those who practice mindfulness regularly. Conversely, the amygdala, which plays a key role in our stress response, often shows reduced activity.

Mindfulness practice also leads to decreased levels of cortisol, the stress hormone, and has been linked to improved immune function. This physiological response contributes to a greater sense of calm and well-being, making mindfulness a valuable tool for managing stress and anxiety.

Benefits of Mindfulness for Teens

For teenagers, the adolescent years can be particularly tumultuous. The pressure to succeed academically, navigate social dynamics, and cope with rapidly changing emotions can be overwhelming. Mindfulness offers several benefits specifically suited to young adults:

1. **Enhanced Emotional Regulation**: Mindfulness helps teens understand and manage their emotions. Instead of being reactive or overwhelmed by feelings like anger, sadness, or anxiety, they learn to observe these emotions without judgment, which can lead to healthier responses.
2. **Reduced Anxiety and Stress**: By practicing mindfulness, teens can experience a decrease in symptoms associated with anxiety and stress. Mindfulness allows them to cultivate a sense of peace and calm in the face of life's challenges.
3. **Improved Focus and Concentration**: With distractions all around—social media, smartphones, and constant notifications—many teens struggle to maintain focus. Mindfulness training can improve concentration and attention, enabling them to engage more fully in their studies and daily activities.
4. **Increased Resilience**: Mindfulness fosters resilience, helping teens bounce back from setbacks and navigate challenges with greater ease. It encourages a growth mindset, where challenges are viewed as opportunities for learning and personal growth.
5. **Better Relationships**: Mindfulness promotes empathy and understanding, improving communication and connection with peers and family. When teens are present and attentive in their interactions, they can build deeper, more meaningful relationships.

How to Practice Mindfulness

Mindfulness is accessible to everyone, regardless of age or background. Here are some practical techniques that teenagers can incorporate into their daily lives to cultivate mindfulness:

1. Mindful Breathing

Mindful breathing is one of the simplest yet most powerful mindfulness techniques. It involves focusing your attention on your breath and observing the sensations of inhaling and exhaling.

How to Practice:

- Find a quiet place where you can sit comfortably.
- Close your eyes and take a deep breath in through your nose, feeling your abdomen expand.
- Hold the breath for a moment, then slowly exhale through your mouth, noticing how your body relaxes.
- Continue to focus on your breath, noticing each inhalation and exhalation.
- If your mind wanders (which it inevitably will), gently bring your attention back to your breath without judgment.

2. Body Scan

The body scan is a technique that encourages you to connect with your physical sensations. This practice can help reduce tension and promote relaxation.

How to Practice:

- Lie down comfortably on your back, with your arms at your sides.
- Close your eyes and take a few deep breaths to settle in.
- Begin by focusing on your toes. Notice any sensations—tension, warmth, or relaxation.
- Gradually move your attention up your body—feet, calves, thighs, hips, abdomen, chest, arms, neck, and head—spending a few moments on each area.
- Acknowledge any areas of tension and consciously relax them as you breathe out.

3. Mindful Observation

Mindful observation invites you to engage with your surroundings by noticing the details of what you see, hear, smell, and feel. It can be done anywhere—while walking, sitting in a café, or even during class.

How to Practice:

- Choose an object in your environment—a flower, a cup, or even the sky.
- Spend a few minutes observing it closely. Notice the colors, shapes, textures, and any other details.
- Allow yourself to become fully absorbed in this observation, tuning out distractions.

4. Gratitude Journaling

Keeping a gratitude journal encourages mindfulness by shifting your focus from negative thoughts to positive experiences. Writing down what you are grateful for can foster a sense of appreciation and presence.

How to Practice:

- Each day, take a few minutes to write down three things you are grateful for.
- They can be as simple as enjoying a sunny day or appreciating a friend's kindness.
- Reflect on why these things are meaningful to you, deepening your connection to positive moments in your life.

5. Mindful Walking

Walking is an everyday activity that can be transformed into a mindfulness practice. Mindful walking encourages you to focus on the sensations of movement and the environment around you.

How to Practice:

- Find a quiet place to walk, whether indoors or outdoors.
- Pay attention to the sensation of your feet touching the ground, the rhythm of your steps, and your breath.
- Notice the sights, sounds, and smells around you as you walk, allowing yourself to fully experience the moment.

Integrating Mindfulness into Daily Life

Incorporating mindfulness into daily life doesn't require hours of practice each day. Small, intentional moments can make a significant impact. Here are some tips for integrating mindfulness into your routine:

- **Set Reminders**: Use your phone or sticky notes to remind yourself to pause and practice mindfulness throughout the day.
- **Mindful Eating**: Take time during meals to savor each bite. Notice the flavors, textures, and aromas of your food.
- **Limit Distractions**: Create tech-free zones or times where you can focus on being present—whether it's during meals or before bedtime.
- **Practice Self-Compassion**: Remember that mindfulness is a skill that takes time to develop. Be gentle with yourself on this journey.

Mindfulness is a powerful tool that can help teenagers navigate the complexities of life with greater ease and confidence. By fostering awareness and acceptance of the present moment, mindfulness empowers young people to manage stress, reduce anxiety, and enhance their overall well-being. As you embark on this mindfulness journey, remember that every moment is an opportunity to practice being present, to cultivate a deeper understanding of yourself and the world around you. The path to mindfulness is a journey, not a destination—embrace each step along the way.

Simple Mindful Breathing and Body Scans

In our fast-paced, often chaotic world, it's all too easy for our minds to get swept away in a torrent of thoughts, worries, and distractions. For teenagers, this experience can be especially overwhelming. As the pressures of school, relationships, and social media pile up, it can feel like you're constantly juggling a million things at once. This is where mindfulness comes into play.

Mindfulness is not just a trendy buzzword; it's a powerful tool that can help you regain control, reduce anxiety, and promote overall well-being. In this chapter, we will explore mindfulness techniques that focus on simple mindful breathing and body scans, two foundational practices that can help you anchor yourself in the present moment.

Understanding Mindfulness

Before diving into the specific techniques, it's essential to understand what mindfulness truly means. Mindfulness is the practice of being fully present in the moment, observing your thoughts, feelings, and bodily sensations without judgment. It encourages you to step out of the whirlwind of your thoughts and into the rich tapestry of your current experience. Mindfulness is not about suppressing your feelings or trying to achieve a state of perpetual calm; rather, it's about recognizing what is happening right now—both internally and externally.

Studies have shown that mindfulness can have profound benefits for mental health, particularly in reducing symptoms of anxiety and depression. By cultivating a mindful awareness, you create space to respond to your thoughts and feelings with greater clarity, rather than reacting impulsively. This chapter will equip you with tools to practice mindfulness through two accessible techniques: mindful breathing and body scans.

Simple Mindful Breathing

Mindful breathing is one of the simplest and most effective ways to anchor yourself in the present moment. It requires no special equipment or lengthy preparation—just you and your breath. Let's explore how to practice this technique step by step.

Step 1: Find Your Space

Start by finding a quiet and comfortable place where you won't be disturbed. It could be your bedroom, a cozy corner of the living room, or even outside in nature. Ensure that you're sitting or lying down in a comfortable position. Allow your body to relax and settle. If you're sitting, keep your back straight but not rigid. If lying down, let your body sink into the surface beneath you.

Step 2: Close Your Eyes

Gently close your eyes or lower your gaze to minimize distractions. This helps turn your focus inward and encourages a sense of calm.

Step 3: Take a Deep Breath

Take a deep breath in through your nose, allowing your abdomen to rise as you fill your lungs with air. Hold this breath for a moment. Then, exhale slowly through your mouth or nose, allowing your body to relax further with each exhale. Repeat this deep breathing two or three times to settle into the rhythm of your breath.

Step 4: Focus on Your Breath

Now, let your breath return to its natural rhythm. Rather than controlling it, simply observe it. Notice the sensation of the air entering and leaving your body. Feel the coolness of the breath as it enters your nostrils and the warmth as it exits. Pay attention to how your chest and abdomen rise and fall. If your mind begins to wander—perhaps to worries about school, friendships, or upcoming events—gently bring your focus back to your breath. It's natural for thoughts to arise; the key is not to engage with them, but simply to acknowledge their presence and return your attention to your breath.

Step 5: Count Your Breaths (Optional)

If you find it challenging to stay focused, try counting your breaths. Inhale deeply and silently count "one" as you breathe in. Exhale and count "two" as you breathe out. Continue counting your breaths up to ten and then start again at one. This technique can help maintain your focus and prevent your mind from wandering too far.

Step 6: Conclude the Practice

After five to ten minutes of mindful breathing, slowly bring your awareness back to your surroundings. Wiggle your fingers and toes, and when you're ready, gently open your eyes. Take a moment to notice how you feel. You may find that you feel calmer, more centered, and better equipped to handle whatever challenges lie ahead.

Body Scans

The body scan is another powerful mindfulness technique that enhances your awareness of physical sensations and helps you release tension. It allows you to connect with your body, recognize areas of discomfort or stress, and cultivate a sense of relaxation. Here's how to do it:

Step 1: Settle into a Comfortable Position

Find a quiet place where you can lie down comfortably. You can lie flat on your back with your arms relaxed by your sides, or you can choose a seated position if that's more comfortable for you. Close your eyes and take a few deep breaths to help you relax.

Step 2: Start with Your Breath

Before beginning the body scan, take a moment to focus on your breath, as you did in the previous exercise. Allow your breath to become a natural rhythm, and take a few moments to feel your body relax with each exhale.

Step 3: Focus on Your Feet

Begin your body scan by bringing your attention to your feet. Notice any sensations—perhaps tingling, warmth, or tension. Allow your feet to relax completely, imagining any tension melting away with each breath.

Step 4: Move Up Through Your Body

Gradually shift your attention upward through your body. Move from your feet to your ankles, calves, knees, thighs, and so on. Spend a few moments on each body part, observing any sensations or tension without judgment. If you notice discomfort, simply acknowledge it and allow it to be present without trying to change it.

Step 5: Continue Through Your Body

Continue this process all the way up to the crown of your head. As you scan each area, visualize sending your breath to that part of your body. Imagine inhaling calmness and exhaling tension. With each breath, feel yourself becoming more relaxed and grounded.

Step 6: Acknowledge Your Emotions

As you perform the body scan, you may also notice emotions or thoughts arising. This is perfectly normal. Acknowledge them without judgment and return your focus to the physical sensations in your body. If you feel emotional pain or discomfort, breathe into that area and allow yourself to simply be with those feelings.

Step 7: Conclude the Practice

Once you've scanned your entire body, take a moment to bring your awareness back to your breath. Take a few deep breaths, feeling the rise and fall of your abdomen. When you're ready, gently open your eyes and take a moment to notice how you feel physically and emotionally.

Benefits of Mindful Breathing and Body Scans

Both mindful breathing and body scans offer numerous benefits, particularly for teenagers navigating the complexities of adolescence. By integrating these practices into your daily routine, you may experience:

- **Reduced Anxiety and Stress**: These techniques help you manage feelings of anxiety and stress by creating a mental space where you can observe your thoughts and feelings without getting overwhelmed.
- **Increased Focus and Concentration**: Mindfulness practices enhance your ability to concentrate on tasks, improving performance in academics and other activities.
- **Better Emotional Regulation**: Regular practice can lead to greater awareness of your emotions, helping you respond to situations more thoughtfully rather than reacting impulsively.
- **Improved Sleep Quality**: Mindfulness can promote relaxation, making it easier to fall asleep and stay asleep, which is crucial for teens needing restorative rest.
- **Greater Self-Acceptance**: As you learn to observe your thoughts and feelings without judgment, you cultivate a more compassionate relationship with yourself, fostering greater self-acceptance.

Integrating Mindfulness into Your Daily Life

To reap the full benefits of these mindfulness techniques, consider incorporating them into your daily routine. You don't need to set aside hours for practice; even a few minutes a day can make a significant difference. Here are some suggestions for integrating mindfulness into your life:

- **Morning Rituals**: Start your day with a few minutes of mindful breathing before getting out of bed. This can help set a positive tone for the day ahead.
- **Mindful Breaks**: During school breaks or study sessions, take short breaks to practice mindful breathing or a quick body scan to recharge your mind and body.
- **Before Sleep**: Establish a calming bedtime routine that includes mindfulness practices. This can help ease the transition into sleep and promote restful nights.
- **Mindfulness in Motion**: Practice mindfulness while walking, eating, or engaging in other activities. Focus on your breath and sensations in your body as you move through your day.

Mindfulness is a powerful tool for managing anxiety and overthinking, particularly for teenagers navigating the tumultuous waters of adolescence. By practicing mindful breathing and body scans, you can cultivate a deeper awareness of yourself and your surroundings, allowing you to respond to life's challenges with greater clarity and resilience. Remember, mindfulness is a skill that takes practice, so be patient with yourself as you explore these techniques. With time, you will discover that being present can transform the way you experience your thoughts and emotions, leading to a more balanced and fulfilling life.

The Power of the Present Moment

In an age defined by rapid technological advancements and a constant flow of information, the concept of the "present moment" can often seem elusive. Our minds are frequently occupied with the past—rehashing old conversations, reliving regrets—or racing toward the future, filled with anxiety about what's to come. This tendency to drift away from the present can be detrimental to our mental health and overall well-being. As a mental health professional, I want to explore the profound impact of embracing the present moment, grounded in mindfulness principles and therapeutic practices.

Understanding the Present Moment

At its core, the present moment refers to the "now"—the space where our thoughts, feelings, and experiences intersect. It's the only moment in which we truly exist. While we can reflect on past experiences or anticipate future events, our actual experiences unfold in the present. This notion is not merely philosophical; it has practical implications for how we live our daily lives.

When we become fully present, we engage with our environment and ourselves in a way that enhances our awareness and appreciation for life. We are more attuned to our thoughts and feelings, allowing us to respond to them thoughtfully rather than react impulsively. This practice can significantly reduce feelings of stress and anxiety, fostering a sense of calm and clarity.

The Science Behind Mindfulness and the Present Moment

Research has shown that practicing mindfulness—being present and fully engaged with the current moment—can have profound effects on mental health. Mindfulness meditation, in particular, has been linked to decreased levels of anxiety, depression, and stress. Studies indicate that regular mindfulness practice can lead to structural changes in the brain, enhancing areas associated with emotional regulation, attention, and self-awareness.

When we engage in mindfulness, we activate the parasympathetic nervous system, which is responsible for our "rest and digest" functions. This activation counters the fight-or-flight response triggered by stress. By focusing on the present moment, we can ground ourselves and reduce feelings of overwhelm, allowing us to navigate life's challenges more effectively.

Overcoming the Barriers to Being Present

While the benefits of being present are clear, many obstacles can hinder our ability to embrace the now. These barriers often manifest as mental distractions, emotional blocks, or even physical discomfort. Let's explore some common challenges individuals face and strategies to overcome them:

1. **The Pull of the Past:**
   Our minds are often drawn to past experiences, particularly those that evoke regret or nostalgia. To combat this tendency, practice self-compassion. Acknowledge your feelings about the past without judgment, and remind yourself that the present moment is where you have the power to create change.

2. **Anxiety About the Future:**
   Worrying about what lies ahead can be paralyzing. To ground yourself, engage in breathing exercises. Deep, intentional breaths can anchor you in the present, allowing you to release future-oriented anxieties. Techniques such as the 4-7-8 breathing method—inhale for 4 seconds, hold for 7 seconds, and exhale for 8 seconds—can help alleviate anxiety and bring you back to the present.

3. **Multitasking and Distraction:**
   In our hyper-connected world, multitasking has become the norm. However, this often leads to fragmented attention and decreased productivity. To counter this, practice single-tasking. Focus on one task at a time, immersing yourself fully in it. This not only enhances your productivity but also fosters a deeper connection to the present moment.

4. **Physical Discomfort:**
   Pain or discomfort can pull us out of the present, diverting our attention to our bodily sensations. Incorporating body scans or gentle stretching into your routine can help you reconnect with your body. These practices enhance awareness and encourage acceptance of physical sensations, allowing you to stay present despite discomfort.

Mindfulness Techniques to Cultivate Presence

Embracing the power of the present moment requires practice and commitment. Here are several mindfulness techniques you can incorporate into your daily life:

1. **Mindful Breathing:**
   Focus on your breath as it flows in and out. Notice the sensations in your nostrils, the rise and fall of your chest, and the rhythm of your breath. Whenever your mind wanders, gently guide it back to the breath. This simple practice can center you in the present moment.

2. **Body Scan Meditation:**
   Lie down comfortably and close your eyes. Starting at the top of your head, slowly bring your awareness to each part of your body, noticing any sensations without judgment. This practice helps cultivate awareness of your body and enhances your connection to the present moment.

3. **Engaging the Senses:**
   Take a moment to focus on your surroundings. What do you see, hear, smell, and feel? Engaging your senses helps ground you in the present. For instance, if you're outside,

notice the colors of the leaves, the sound of birds, and the feel of the breeze against your skin.

4. **Mindful Walking:**
   When you walk, pay attention to each step. Notice how your foot lifts, moves through the air, and lands on the ground. Focus on the sensations in your legs and feet. This practice can transform a mundane activity into a mindful experience.

5. **Gratitude Journaling:**
   At the end of each day, take a few moments to reflect on three things you are grateful for. This practice not only enhances your mood but also encourages you to appreciate the present moment and the positive aspects of your life.

The Transformative Effects of Living in the Now

When we commit to living in the present, we open ourselves to a multitude of benefits. Emotionally, we experience a reduction in anxiety and stress as we learn to accept our thoughts and feelings without judgment. We cultivate resilience, enhancing our ability to cope with challenges and uncertainties.

Socially, being present fosters deeper connections with others. When we engage fully in conversations, we become better listeners, creating more meaningful interactions. This presence not only enhances our relationships but also contributes to our overall sense of belonging and fulfillment.

Spiritually, embracing the present moment can lead to a greater sense of purpose and authenticity. We begin to recognize the beauty in everyday experiences, finding joy in the simple act of being. This connection to the now can foster a sense of gratitude for life, leading to improved overall well-being.

The power of the present moment is a profound tool for enhancing mental health and well-being. As you embark on this journey toward mindfulness, remember that it is not about achieving perfection but about cultivating awareness and acceptance of each moment as it comes.

Start small—incorporate mindfulness practices into your daily routine and gradually increase your awareness of the present. As you do so, you will likely notice shifts in your emotional landscape, relationships, and overall quality of life. The present moment is a gift; by learning to embrace it, you open the door to a more fulfilling, vibrant existence.

Remember, it's not just about being present; it's about truly **living** in the moment. With practice, you can transform the way you experience life, shifting from a state of constant distraction to one of focused awareness and connection. Embrace the power of the present moment, and watch as your world transforms around you.

Chapter 4: Challenging Negative Thoughts

Reframing and Cognitive Behavioral Techniques

In the landscape of our thoughts, negativity can often feel like an unwelcome guest who overstays their welcome. For teenagers navigating the tumultuous waters of adolescence, negative thoughts can be particularly insidious. They can weave through the mind like a persistent echo, creating a feedback loop that amplifies anxiety, low self-esteem, and feelings of inadequacy. However, by understanding how to challenge these thoughts—through reframing and cognitive behavioral techniques—young adults can reclaim their mental space and foster a more balanced perspective on life.

The Nature of Negative Thoughts

Before we dive into strategies for challenging negative thoughts, it's crucial to understand their nature. Negative thoughts can manifest in various forms, such as self-doubt, catastrophic thinking, or harsh self-criticism. For example, a teenager might think, "I'm terrible at math; I'll never understand it," after receiving a poor grade. This thought can spiral into feelings of hopelessness, leading to avoidance of studying altogether.

These negative thoughts often arise from cognitive distortions—systematic errors in thinking that can lead to misinterpretations of reality. Some common distortions include:

- **All-or-Nothing Thinking**: Viewing situations in black-and-white terms without recognizing the gray areas. For example, thinking, "If I don't get an A, I'm a failure."
- **Overgeneralization**: Making broad conclusions based on a single event. For instance, believing, "I messed up one presentation, so I always mess up."
- **Catastrophizing**: Expecting the worst possible outcome in a situation. This might look like thinking, "If I fail this test, I won't get into college."

These thought patterns are not just simple misjudgments; they are deeply ingrained habits of thinking that can significantly impact a teenager's self-image and mental health.

The Power of Reframing

Reframing is a powerful technique that involves changing the way we perceive a situation. Instead of getting stuck in a negative thought spiral, reframing encourages us to view the situation from a different angle—one that is more constructive and less distressing.

How to Reframe Negative Thoughts

1. **Awareness**: The first step in reframing is awareness. Pay attention to your thoughts, especially those that lead to feelings of anxiety or self-doubt. Keep a thought diary where you jot down negative thoughts as they arise. Recognizing these thoughts is vital to addressing them.
2. **Question Your Thoughts**: Once you've identified a negative thought, challenge its validity. Ask yourself questions like:
    - What evidence do I have that supports this thought?
    - Is there evidence that contradicts this thought?
    - Am I viewing this situation objectively, or am I letting emotions cloud my judgment?
3. **Find Alternative Explanations**: Instead of accepting a negative thought at face value, try to find alternative explanations. For instance, if you think, "I'm bad at making friends," consider other possibilities:
    - "I'm still getting used to this new school."
    - "I've made a few connections; it just takes time."
    - "Making friends can be challenging for everyone."
4. **Use Positive Affirmations**: Replace negative thoughts with positive affirmations. When you catch yourself thinking, "I can't handle this," reframe it to, "I can learn how to handle this, one step at a time." Positive affirmations help reinforce a more balanced perspective and counteract negative self-talk.
5. **Visualize Success**: Visualization is a powerful tool in reframing. Picture yourself successfully navigating a challenging situation. Imagine the steps you would take and how you would feel. This mental rehearsal can create a more positive outlook and reduce anxiety about upcoming events.

Cognitive Behavioral Techniques

Cognitive Behavioral Therapy (CBT) is a structured approach that helps individuals identify and challenge negative thought patterns. It emphasizes the connection between thoughts, feelings, and behaviors, illustrating how distorted thinking can lead to emotional distress. Here are several key techniques derived from CBT that can help teens combat negative thoughts:

1. Thought Records

Thought records are a practical tool for tracking negative thoughts and challenging them systematically. Here's how to create one:

- **Situation**: Write down the situation that triggered the negative thought.
- **Emotion**: Identify the emotions you felt and rate their intensity (on a scale from 1 to 10).
- **Negative Thought**: Record the negative thought you had.
- **Evidence For and Against**: List evidence that supports the thought and evidence that contradicts it.

- **Reframed Thought**: Create a balanced thought that takes into account the evidence you've gathered.

This structured approach helps clarify your thought process and encourages a more rational evaluation of situations.

2. Behavioral Experiments

Behavioral experiments involve testing the validity of negative thoughts through real-life experiences. For instance, if a teenager believes, "If I speak up in class, everyone will laugh at me," they could conduct an experiment by volunteering to answer a question. After the experience, they can reflect on the outcome: Was their fear accurate? How did their classmates respond? This technique allows individuals to gather evidence to challenge their distorted beliefs.

3. Exposure Techniques

For some, the mere thought of certain situations—like public speaking or social gatherings—can trigger overwhelming anxiety. Exposure techniques involve gradually facing these fears in a controlled way, starting with less intimidating scenarios and gradually increasing the level of challenge. This process helps desensitize individuals to their fears and reduces the power these negative thoughts hold over them.

4. Mindfulness Practices

Incorporating mindfulness practices can significantly enhance the effectiveness of reframing and cognitive behavioral techniques. Mindfulness encourages individuals to observe their thoughts without judgment, creating a space between their thoughts and their reactions. This practice can reduce the intensity of negative thoughts and enhance emotional regulation. Techniques include:

- **Mindful Breathing**: Focus on your breath, noticing the inhalation and exhalation. When negative thoughts arise, acknowledge them, and let them pass without engaging.
- **Body Scan Meditation**: Practice bringing awareness to different parts of your body, which can ground you in the present moment and reduce anxiety.

Challenging negative thoughts through reframing and cognitive behavioral techniques can empower teenagers to take control of their mental well-being. By fostering awareness, questioning distorted thoughts, and utilizing structured techniques, they can develop a healthier, more balanced perspective.

It's important to remember that this is a skill that requires practice. As with any new habit, consistency is key. Encourage yourself to embrace this journey, knowing that every step taken toward challenging negative thoughts is a step toward a brighter, more hopeful outlook. Just like any skill worth mastering, it takes time and patience, but the rewards of reduced anxiety, improved self-esteem, and a more positive self-image are well worth the effort.

In this ever-changing world, where stressors can feel overwhelming, equipping ourselves with tools to challenge negative thoughts is not just beneficial—it's essential for nurturing mental health and resilience in the face of life's challenges.

Productive vs. Unproductive Thinking

When it comes to our thoughts, not all mental chatter is created equal. Some thoughts help us navigate our world and push us towards growth, while others can trap us in a cycle of negativity and despair. This chapter is dedicated to helping you identify, challenge, and reshape your thinking patterns, transforming unproductive thoughts into productive ones that foster resilience and well-being.

Understanding the Nature of Thoughts

Before diving into the specifics of productive and unproductive thinking, it's crucial to understand what thoughts are. Thoughts are mental events—fleeting images, ideas, or notions—that arise in our minds in response to stimuli from the world around us. They can be influenced by our emotions, experiences, beliefs, and even our environment. The problem arises when certain thoughts, particularly those that are negative, become pervasive and begin to dictate our feelings and behaviors.

The Cost of Unproductive Thinking

Unproductive thinking, often characterized by negative self-talk, ruminative thought patterns, or catastrophic thinking, can have detrimental effects on your mental health. When we engage in this type of thinking, we can feel trapped, anxious, and overwhelmed. Here are some common forms of unproductive thinking:

1. **Catastrophizing**: This is the tendency to expect the worst possible outcome in any given situation. For example, if you don't perform well on a test, you might think, "I'll never get into college; my life is ruined." Catastrophizing amplifies fear and anxiety, often leading to paralysis in decision-making.
2. **All-or-Nothing Thinking**: This black-and-white mindset leaves no room for nuance. You might think, "If I don't get an A on this assignment, I'm a complete failure." This kind of thinking can create a sense of hopelessness, as you focus solely on extremes rather than recognizing the middle ground.
3. **Overgeneralization**: This occurs when one negative experience leads you to believe that every situation will turn out the same way. For instance, "I embarrassed myself at that

party, so I will always embarrass myself in social situations." Overgeneralization can lead to isolation and avoidance behaviors.

4. **Should Statements**: These are rigid and unrealistic expectations we place on ourselves, like "I should always be happy" or "I should never make mistakes." Such thoughts can generate feelings of guilt and inadequacy when we inevitably fall short of these impossible standards.

5. **Mind Reading**: This involves assuming you know what others are thinking, often leading to unwarranted anxiety. For example, "She didn't respond to my text; she must think I'm annoying." This type of thinking can create unnecessary tension in relationships.

Understanding these patterns is the first step in challenging and changing them. Unproductive thoughts can spiral out of control, leading to anxiety, depression, and low self-esteem. However, the good news is that we can learn to disrupt these patterns through conscious effort and mindfulness.

The Power of Productive Thinking

Productive thinking, on the other hand, involves thoughts that are constructive and empowering. They help you problem-solve, cope with challenges, and foster a sense of agency over your life. Here are characteristics of productive thinking:

1. **Realistic Assessments**: Instead of jumping to worst-case scenarios, productive thinkers analyze situations objectively. They might say, "I didn't do well on this test, but I can study harder for the next one." This promotes a growth mindset.

2. **Flexibility**: Productive thinkers embrace nuance. They recognize that life is complex and that it's okay to have mixed feelings about a situation. Instead of "I failed," they might think, "I learned something valuable from this experience."

3. **Constructive Self-Talk**: Productive thinkers engage in positive self-talk, which can be affirming and motivating. For instance, instead of "I'm terrible at this," they might say, "I'm still learning, and it's okay to make mistakes."

4. **Focus on Solutions**: Rather than dwelling on problems, productive thinkers shift their focus to potential solutions. If a friend cancels plans, they might think, "Let's find another time to hang out" instead of feeling rejected.

5. **Gratitude and Positivity**: Productive thinking often includes an awareness of the positive aspects of life. Cultivating gratitude can counteract negative thoughts and help maintain perspective.

Challenging Unproductive Thoughts

To shift from unproductive to productive thinking, we must actively challenge our negative thoughts. This process can be broken down into several steps:

1. Awareness

The first step in challenging negative thoughts is becoming aware of them. Keep a journal where you jot down negative thoughts as they arise. This practice helps you recognize patterns in your thinking. You might notice that certain situations trigger similar negative thoughts, making them easier to address over time.

2. Questioning Your Thoughts

Once you identify negative thoughts, ask yourself a series of questions to challenge their validity:

- **Is this thought based on facts or assumptions?**
- **What evidence do I have that supports or contradicts this thought?**
- **How would I respond if a friend were thinking this way?**
- **What would I tell my best friend if they expressed this thought?**

This cognitive restructuring process helps you develop a more balanced perspective.

3. Reframing

Reframing is the practice of changing your perspective on a thought. For example, if you think, "I'm going to embarrass myself in this presentation," try reframing it to, "I might feel nervous, but I can prepare and do my best." This shift opens up possibilities for a more positive outcome.

4. Practice Mindfulness

Mindfulness is the practice of being present in the moment without judgment. By engaging in mindfulness meditation or simple breathing exercises, you can learn to observe your thoughts without getting caught up in them. This distance can help you recognize that thoughts are just thoughts—they don't have to dictate your emotions or actions.

5. Create Positive Affirmations

Positive affirmations are statements that can help reshape your thinking. Create affirmations that counteract your negative thoughts. For example, if you struggle with perfectionism, an affirmation might be, "I am doing my best, and that is enough." Repeat these affirmations daily to reinforce positive thinking patterns.

6. Seek Feedback

Sometimes, sharing your thoughts with trusted friends, family, or a therapist can provide valuable perspective. They can help you see situations more clearly and offer alternative viewpoints. This external feedback can be instrumental in breaking the cycle of negative thinking.

Practicing Productive Thinking in Daily Life

Now that you have tools for challenging negative thoughts, it's important to integrate productive thinking into your daily routine. Here are some strategies to consider:

1. **Daily Reflection**: Set aside time each day to reflect on your thoughts. Identify any unproductive thoughts and consciously work to reframe them into productive ones. This practice builds awareness and helps reinforce new thought patterns.
2. **Gratitude Journaling**: Each evening, write down three things you are grateful for that day. Focusing on gratitude can help shift your mindset and promote positivity.
3. **Set Intentions**: Start your day with positive intentions. For example, you might say, "Today, I will approach challenges with a growth mindset," or "I will practice kindness towards myself."
4. **Limit Negative Inputs**: Be mindful of the media you consume, including social media. Surround yourself with positive influences and limit exposure to negative or toxic environments.
5. **Engage in Activities that Foster Growth**: Pursue hobbies, interests, and activities that challenge you and encourage personal development. Engaging in such activities helps build resilience and confidence.

Challenging negative thoughts is a journey, and it requires practice, patience, and self-compassion. By learning to identify unproductive thinking patterns and actively replacing them with constructive thoughts, you empower yourself to navigate life's challenges with greater confidence and clarity. Remember, the goal isn't to eliminate all negative thoughts but to develop a healthier relationship with your mind. With practice, you can cultivate a mindset that not only withstands the storms of anxiety and overthinking but thrives amidst them.

By embracing productive thinking, you open the door to a more fulfilling and meaningful life—one where you can tackle obstacles head-on, embrace your true self, and live authentically. Your thoughts shape your reality; let them reflect your strengths, hopes, and the limitless possibilities ahead.

Using Mindfulness to Tackle Catastrophizing

Catastrophizing is a cognitive distortion characterized by the tendency to anticipate the worst possible outcomes in any given situation. For many individuals, especially teenagers facing the pressures of school, social interactions, and self-identity, this thinking pattern can lead to heightened anxiety and stress. It can feel as though your mind is perpetually stuck in a loop of "what ifs," spiraling into an overwhelming sense of dread. Fortunately, mindfulness offers practical tools to counteract this negative thinking pattern. By anchoring ourselves in the present moment, we can mitigate the grip of catastrophizing and foster a more balanced perspective.

Understanding Catastrophizing

Before we delve into mindfulness techniques, it's crucial to understand the nature of catastrophizing. This cognitive distortion often manifests as an automatic thought pattern, where individuals leap to the worst-case scenario without sufficient evidence. For instance, if a student receives a low grade on a test, they might think, "I'm going to fail this class, ruin my GPA, and never get into college!" This type of thinking is not only unhelpful but also unfounded, as it overlooks the full range of possible outcomes and the individual's capacity for recovery and growth.

Research has shown that catastrophizing can lead to increased feelings of helplessness, depression, and anxiety. By habitually anticipating disaster, individuals set themselves up for unnecessary emotional turmoil. The good news is that mindfulness techniques can help disrupt this cycle of negative thinking and promote a more realistic and compassionate perspective.

Mindfulness Techniques to Combat Catastrophizing

1. Mindful Breathing

Mindful breathing is a fundamental mindfulness technique that can be practiced anywhere and at any time. Here's how to get started:

- **Find a Comfortable Position:** Sit or lie down in a comfortable position. Close your eyes if you feel comfortable doing so.
- **Focus on Your Breath:** Take a deep breath in through your nose, allowing your abdomen to rise. Hold for a moment, and then exhale slowly through your mouth. Notice the sensation of the air entering and leaving your body.
- **Count Your Breaths:** To maintain focus, you can count each inhale and exhale. Inhale (1), exhale (2), and so forth, up to 10. Then, start over. If your mind begins to wander to catastrophic thoughts, gently acknowledge this and redirect your focus back to your breath.
- **Practice Regularly:** Try to practice mindful breathing for a few minutes daily. Over time, you'll find that it becomes easier to center yourself when faced with anxious thoughts.

2. Body Scan Meditation

The body scan meditation is another effective technique for reducing anxiety and grounding yourself in the present moment. This practice helps you connect with your body and release tension associated with catastrophic thinking.

- **Lie Down Comfortably:** Find a quiet space and lie down flat on your back, arms resting comfortably at your sides.
- **Begin at Your Toes:** Close your eyes and take a few deep breaths. Then, shift your attention to your toes. Notice any sensations, tension, or discomfort.
- **Move Upward:** Gradually move your focus up through your feet, ankles, calves, knees, thighs, and so on. Spend a few moments at each body part, observing any sensations or feelings.
- **Release Tension:** If you notice tension, consciously relax that area. Visualize your breath flowing into that part of your body, releasing the tension as you exhale.
- **Acknowledge Your Thoughts:** If catastrophic thoughts arise during this process, acknowledge them without judgment. Remind yourself that thoughts are just thoughts; they do not define reality.

3. Mindful Observation

This technique encourages you to observe your surroundings with curiosity and wonder, shifting your focus away from internal anxiety to the external world.

- **Choose an Object:** Select an object in your environment—this could be anything from a plant to a piece of furniture.
- **Engage Your Senses:** Spend a few moments observing the object. Notice its color, shape, texture, and size. What sounds do you hear around it? What scents do you notice? Engaging multiple senses can ground you in the present and distract you from catastrophic thinking.
- **Reflect on Your Experience:** After a few minutes, take a moment to reflect on the experience. Did this practice change how you felt about your catastrophic thoughts?

4. Journaling and Thought Records

Writing can be a powerful tool for managing anxious thoughts and gaining clarity. Keeping a journal allows you to externalize your thoughts, making it easier to challenge and reframe them.

- **Identify Your Thoughts:** When you find yourself catastrophizing, take a moment to write down your thoughts. Be specific about the scenario you're envisioning.
- **Evaluate the Evidence:** Next to each catastrophic thought, write down evidence for and against that thought. For example, if you wrote, "I will fail this class," counter it with, "I studied hard, and I have passed other tests before."

- **Reframe Your Thoughts:** Use your evaluation to reframe your catastrophic thinking. Instead of "I'm going to fail," you might say, "I can learn from this experience and do better next time."
- **Reflect on Progress:** Regularly revisit your journal entries to see how your thinking has evolved over time. Acknowledging progress can bolster self-compassion and resilience.

5. Mindfulness Apps and Guided Meditations

Incorporating technology can enhance your mindfulness practice. Numerous apps offer guided meditations specifically designed to combat anxiety and foster mindfulness. Here are a few popular options:

- **Headspace:** This app provides a range of guided meditations and mindfulness exercises, including sessions focused on anxiety and overthinking.
- **Calm:** Calm offers various meditations, sleep stories, and relaxing music, with a specific focus on mindfulness and emotional regulation.
- **Insight Timer:** A vast library of guided meditations from various instructors allows users to explore different techniques and find what resonates with them.

6. Practice Gratitude

Mindfulness is not just about awareness; it's also about cultivating a positive mindset. Practicing gratitude can shift your focus from what's wrong to what's good in your life.

- **Daily Gratitude List:** Each day, write down three things you're grateful for. These can be small or significant, from a good meal to supportive friends.
- **Reflect on the Positive:** When you find yourself catastrophizing, revisit your gratitude list. This practice can help ground you in the present and remind you of the positives in your life.

Integrating Mindfulness into Daily Life

Mindfulness is most effective when integrated into your daily routine. Here are some practical tips for incorporating mindfulness into your life to combat catastrophizing:

1. **Start Small:** Begin with a few minutes of mindfulness each day. Gradually increase the duration as you become more comfortable with the practice.
2. **Be Consistent:** Set aside a specific time each day for mindfulness. Consistency helps reinforce the habit and allows you to experience its benefits over time.
3. **Mindful Moments:** Look for opportunities to practice mindfulness throughout your day. This can be during mundane tasks like washing dishes or walking to school. Focus on the sensations, sights, and sounds around you.

4. **Be Patient:** Mindfulness is a skill that takes time to develop. Be patient with yourself as you navigate this journey, and recognize that setbacks are a natural part of the process.
5. **Seek Support:** Consider joining a mindfulness group or seeking guidance from a mental health professional. Having a supportive community can enhance your practice and provide accountability.

Catastrophizing can create an unending cycle of anxiety and stress, particularly for teenagers grappling with various life pressures. By incorporating mindfulness techniques into your daily routine, you can break free from this cycle and cultivate a more balanced, compassionate perspective. Remember that it's normal to have anxious thoughts; the goal is not to eliminate them but to change your relationship with them. With practice and patience, mindfulness can help you navigate the challenges of life with greater resilience, clarity, and peace. Embrace the journey toward self-discovery and empowerment, knowing that you have the tools to tackle catastrophizing head-on.

Chapter 5: Managing Social Anxiety and Peer Pressure

Navigating Social Media and Peer Expectations

As a teenager, navigating the complexities of social dynamics can be daunting. The pressure to fit in, to be liked, and to be 'in the know' often feels overwhelming. This chapter will explore the relationship between social anxiety, peer pressure, and social media, providing you with strategies to manage these challenges effectively. By understanding these elements and developing coping mechanisms, you can cultivate a sense of self that is resilient, confident, and authentic.

Understanding Social Anxiety

Social anxiety is more than just shyness; it is a persistent fear of social situations that may lead to embarrassment or humiliation. For many teens, this anxiety can stem from various factors, including past experiences, negative self-perceptions, or even the pressures of societal expectations. When faced with situations such as public speaking, meeting new people, or even attending a party, feelings of dread, self-doubt, and nervousness can arise, making it difficult to engage fully in life.

Common Symptoms of Social Anxiety

1. **Physical Symptoms**: These may include sweating, trembling, rapid heartbeat, or nausea. You might find your mind racing, your thoughts muddled, or your body feeling heavy as if it's trying to escape.
2. **Emotional Symptoms**: These can range from overwhelming feelings of fear and worry to pervasive feelings of inadequacy and loneliness. You may feel like you are constantly being judged or that you don't belong.
3. **Behavioral Symptoms**: Avoidance is a common coping mechanism. You might decline invitations to social events, avoid making eye contact, or choose to isolate yourself rather than face potentially uncomfortable situations.

The Role of Peer Pressure

Peer pressure can significantly impact teenagers' mental health. It encompasses the influence your peers have on your behaviors, choices, and self-esteem. While it can motivate positive behaviors, such as studying or participating in sports, it can also lead to negative outcomes, including substance abuse, risky behaviors, and compromising your values.

Types of Peer Pressure

1. **Direct Pressure**: This involves explicit requests or demands from friends to engage in specific behaviors. For example, a friend might urge you to skip class or try smoking, putting you in a difficult position.
2. **Indirect Pressure**: This is subtler, often stemming from observing your peers engage in certain behaviors. The feeling that "everyone else is doing it" can lead to anxiety about not fitting in or being left out.
3. **Self-Imposed Pressure**: Often, the most challenging type of pressure comes from within. You might set high expectations for yourself, believing you must excel in all areas to be accepted. This can lead to self-criticism and anxiety about meeting these unrealistic standards.

Social Media: A Double-Edged Sword

Social media has revolutionized the way teens connect, communicate, and share experiences. Platforms like Instagram, Snapchat, and TikTok allow for instant communication and connection, but they also contribute to increased anxiety and peer pressure. Here are some ways social media can amplify these feelings:

1. **Curated Perceptions**: Social media often presents a filtered version of reality, where only the highlights of life are shared. This can lead to feelings of inadequacy when comparing your everyday life to the seemingly perfect lives of others.
2. **Validation through Likes**: The quest for likes and comments can create a sense of worth based on external validation. If a post doesn't receive the expected response, it may trigger feelings of rejection and anxiety.
3. **Fear of Missing Out (FOMO)**: Seeing friends hang out without you can intensify feelings of loneliness and social exclusion. FOMO can compel you to attend events or engage in activities you might not feel comfortable with, simply to avoid feeling left out.

Strategies to Manage Social Anxiety and Peer Pressure

1. Cultivate Self-Awareness

Begin by recognizing your feelings of anxiety and the triggers that exacerbate them. Journaling can be a useful tool for this. Write about situations that cause anxiety, how you feel in those moments, and what thoughts run through your mind. Understanding your patterns can help you develop strategies to manage your anxiety effectively.

2. Challenge Negative Thoughts

When you experience anxiety, it often stems from negative self-talk. Challenge these thoughts by asking yourself:

- What evidence do I have that supports or contradicts this thought?
- How would I respond to a friend who had this thought?
- Is there a more balanced or positive way to view this situation?

By reframing your thoughts, you can reduce their emotional grip.

3. Set Realistic Expectations

It's essential to recognize that nobody is perfect. Set realistic expectations for yourself and understand that it's okay to make mistakes. Acknowledge that not every social interaction will go flawlessly, and that's part of being human. Embrace imperfections, both in yourself and others.

4. Practice Mindfulness

Mindfulness can help ground you in the present moment, reducing feelings of anxiety. Techniques such as deep breathing, meditation, or mindful observation can be effective. For example, when you feel anxious about a social situation, take a moment to focus on your breath, inhale deeply for a count of four, hold for four, and exhale for four. Repeat this several times to center yourself.

5. Limit Social Media Exposure

Consider taking breaks from social media. Curate your feed to include positive influences and unfollow accounts that make you feel inadequate. When you engage with social media, remind yourself that what you see is often a highlight reel, not the full picture.

6. Find Your Tribe

Surround yourself with supportive friends who appreciate you for who you are. Healthy friendships can help counteract peer pressure and provide a safe space for expressing your feelings. Don't be afraid to communicate your struggles; you may find that others share similar feelings.

7. Role-Playing and Exposure

Gradually expose yourself to social situations that cause anxiety. Start with smaller, less intimidating interactions, such as making small talk with a classmate or attending a gathering with a close friend. Practicing these interactions can build your confidence over time. Role-playing potential scenarios with a trusted friend or family member can also prepare you for real-life situations.

Seeking Professional Help

If you find that your social anxiety is significantly impacting your daily life, consider seeking support from a mental health professional. Therapists can provide strategies tailored to your unique situation and help you navigate your feelings. Cognitive Behavioral Therapy (CBT), for example, is an effective approach for managing anxiety by helping you understand and change negative thought patterns.

Navigating social anxiety and peer pressure can be challenging, but it's important to remember that you are not alone. Many teens experience similar feelings, and it's okay to seek support. By cultivating self-awareness, practicing mindfulness, and building a strong support system, you can learn to manage your anxiety effectively.

As you navigate the complexities of social interactions and social media, focus on embracing your authentic self. Remember that you are worthy of acceptance and love, just as you are. By fostering a sense of self-compassion and understanding, you can transform the pressures of adolescence into opportunities for personal growth and resilience.

Building Confidence in Social Settings

Navigating the maze of social interactions can feel like a daunting task for many teenagers. Whether it's the fear of judgment, the pressure to fit in, or the dread of being misunderstood, social anxiety can often loom large in the lives of young adults. This chapter aims to provide you with practical tools and insights to help you build confidence in social settings and manage the pressures that often accompany them.

Key Characteristics of Social Anxiety:

- **Physical Symptoms:** You may notice a racing heart, sweating, trembling, or a dry mouth when faced with social situations. These physical manifestations can intensify feelings of anxiety.
- **Cognitive Distortions:** Overthinking scenarios, imagining the worst possible outcomes, and engaging in negative self-talk can perpetuate anxiety. Thoughts like "What if I embarrass myself?" or "Everyone will laugh at me" can be paralyzing.
- **Behavioral Avoidance:** To avoid discomfort, you might skip social gatherings or avoid speaking up in class. While this might provide temporary relief, it reinforces anxiety over time.

Strategies for Building Confidence

1. Challenge Your Thoughts

One of the most powerful tools at your disposal is the ability to challenge negative thoughts. Cognitive-behavioral therapy (CBT) techniques can be beneficial here. Start by identifying the anxious thoughts that arise in social situations. Ask yourself:

- **Is this thought based on facts or assumptions?**
- **What evidence do I have to support or refute this thought?**
- **What would I say to a friend who had this thought?**

By reframing your thoughts, you can change your emotional response to social situations. Instead of thinking, "Everyone will notice I'm nervous," you might reframe it to, "Most people are focused on themselves and won't even notice my nerves."

2. Gradual Exposure

Exposure therapy is a common technique used to help individuals confront their fears in a safe and controlled manner. Start with less intimidating social situations and gradually work your way up to more challenging ones. For example:

- **Step 1:** Initiate a conversation with a classmate.
- **Step 2:** Attend a small gathering with close friends.
- **Step 3:** Join a club or group where you can meet new people with shared interests.

By slowly exposing yourself to social situations, you'll build confidence over time. Each successful interaction reinforces your belief in your social abilities, making future situations feel more manageable.

3. Practice Active Listening

Focusing on others during conversations can alleviate some of the pressure you may feel. Instead of worrying about what to say next, engage in active listening. This involves:

- Making eye contact and nodding to show understanding.
- Asking follow-up questions to demonstrate interest.
- Reflecting on what the other person has said before responding.

Active listening shifts the focus away from you, making social interactions feel less daunting. It also helps you connect with others more meaningfully, fostering a sense of belonging.

4. Develop Social Skills Through Role-Playing

Role-playing can be an effective way to practice social interactions in a safe environment. You can do this with a trusted friend, family member, or therapist. Simulate different social scenarios, such as:

- Introducing yourself to someone new.
- Navigating small talk at a party.
- Handling an awkward situation gracefully.

Role-playing allows you to experiment with various responses and behaviors, helping you feel more prepared for real-life situations. It can also reduce anxiety by desensitizing you to potential challenges.

5. Embrace Imperfection

Perfectionism can be a significant barrier to social confidence. The desire to say the perfect thing or make an impeccable first impression can create immense pressure. Embracing imperfection means accepting that mistakes are a natural part of being human.

Consider the Following:

- **Everyone Makes Mistakes:** Remember that even the most confident individuals stumble over their words or experience awkward moments. It's a universal experience.
- **Focus on Connection, Not Performance:** Shift your mindset from "I need to impress" to "I want to connect." Building relationships is more about genuine interactions than performing flawlessly.
- **Practice Self-Compassion:** Be kind to yourself when things don't go as planned. Acknowledge your efforts, and treat yourself with the same understanding you would offer a friend.

Coping with Peer Pressure

Peer pressure can be particularly challenging during adolescence, as the desire to fit in often competes with your personal values and preferences. Here are strategies to help you navigate peer pressure:

1. Know Your Values

Take the time to reflect on what is important to you. Understanding your values provides a solid foundation for decision-making. When faced with peer pressure, ask yourself:

- **Does this align with my values?**
- **Am I comfortable with this choice?**
- **What are the potential consequences?**

Having a clear sense of your values can empower you to stand firm against negative influences.

2. Practice Assertiveness

Being assertive means expressing your thoughts and feelings confidently while respecting others. Practice saying "no" or expressing disagreement in a respectful way. Some assertive responses might include:

- "I appreciate the invite, but I'd rather not."
- "Thanks for the suggestion, but I'm not interested in that."
- "I feel uncomfortable with that; can we do something else?"

Using "I" statements can also be effective. For example, "I feel overwhelmed when…" This helps communicate your feelings without sounding accusatory.

3. Seek Supportive Friends

Surrounding yourself with friends who share your values and respect your boundaries can significantly impact your confidence. Supportive friendships can buffer against peer pressure and encourage positive behaviors.

Look for Friends Who:

- Share similar interests and values.
- Respect your decisions and boundaries.
- Encourage you to be your authentic self.

Building a Resilient Mindset

Building confidence in social settings is a process that takes time and practice. Embrace the journey, and recognize that setbacks are part of growth. Here are some additional tips to help you develop resilience:

- **Set Realistic Goals:** Establish small, achievable social goals. Celebrate your successes, no matter how minor they may seem.
- **Practice Mindfulness:** Mindfulness techniques can help ground you in the present moment, reducing anxiety and enhancing focus during social interactions.
- **Reflect on Experiences:** After social events, take time to reflect on what went well and what you might want to improve. This can help you identify patterns and build a strategy for future interactions.

Building confidence in social settings is an essential skill that will serve you well throughout life. By understanding the roots of social anxiety, challenging negative thoughts, and practicing effective strategies, you can learn to navigate social interactions with greater ease and assurance. Remember that it's perfectly okay to feel nervous; it's a common human experience. With time, patience, and practice, you can cultivate a sense of confidence that allows you to engage meaningfully with others, resist negative peer pressure, and enjoy the rich tapestry of social relationships that life has to offer. Embrace each interaction as an opportunity for growth, and take pride in the progress you make along the way.

Overcoming Fear of Judgment

The fear of judgment is a common experience that many people, especially teenagers and young adults, grapple with. This fear can manifest in various forms: anxiety in social situations, reluctance to express oneself, or avoidance of activities where one feels they might be scrutinized. At its core, the fear of judgment stems from a deep-seated concern about how others perceive us. It can be paralyzing, preventing individuals from pursuing their passions, engaging in social interactions, or even expressing their opinions.

The Roots of Judgment Anxiety

To effectively overcome this fear, it's essential to understand its origins. Fear of judgment can arise from several factors:

1. **Social Conditioning**: From an early age, individuals are conditioned to seek approval from others. This desire for acceptance can lead to an unhealthy focus on how one is perceived. School environments, family dynamics, and social circles can all reinforce the need to conform to specific standards, creating anxiety around the possibility of judgment.
2. **Past Experiences**: Negative experiences, such as criticism or bullying, can leave lasting impressions. A single hurtful comment can instill a fear that similar judgments will recur, leading to heightened sensitivity in future interactions.
3. **Perfectionism**: Individuals with perfectionist tendencies often fear judgment because they hold themselves to unrealistically high standards. This fear can create a cycle of avoidance and self-criticism, as they may feel that any misstep will lead to harsh evaluations from others.
4. **Self-Esteem Issues**: Low self-esteem can exacerbate the fear of judgment. If individuals do not feel confident in their abilities or worth, they may project their insecurities onto others, anticipating negative evaluations.

Recognizing the Impact of Fear of Judgment

The fear of judgment can have a profound impact on an individual's life. It can lead to:

- **Avoidance of Social Situations**: Those who fear judgment may decline invitations to parties, group activities, or public speaking events. This avoidance can result in social isolation and missed opportunities for connection.

- **Inhibition of Self-Expression**: Fear can stifle creativity and self-expression. Individuals may hesitate to share their thoughts, ideas, or talents for fear of being judged, which can inhibit personal growth.
- **Anxiety and Stress**: The constant worry about how one is perceived can lead to heightened anxiety and stress levels. Individuals may experience physical symptoms such as increased heart rate, sweating, or difficulty concentrating.
- **Negative Self-Talk**: The fear of judgment often leads to a pattern of negative self-talk, where individuals criticize themselves and their abilities. This internal dialogue can further damage self-esteem and perpetuate the cycle of fear.

Strategies to Overcome the Fear of Judgment

Overcoming the fear of judgment requires intentional effort and practice. Here are several strategies that can help individuals confront and diminish their fears:

1. Challenge Negative Thoughts

Cognitive Behavioral Therapy (CBT) is an effective approach to address the fear of judgment. Begin by identifying negative thoughts that arise in social situations. Are you worried about how others perceive your outfit? Do you fear that your opinions will be dismissed? Once you identify these thoughts, challenge their validity. Ask yourself questions such as:

- Is there concrete evidence to support this thought?
- What would I say to a friend who feels this way?
- How likely is it that the worst-case scenario will happen?

By reframing these thoughts, individuals can develop a more balanced perspective.

2. Practice Self-Compassion

Developing self-compassion can significantly reduce the fear of judgment. Instead of being harsh on oneself for perceived shortcomings, practice kindness and understanding. Acknowledge that everyone makes mistakes and experiences judgment. Consider keeping a journal to document moments when you feel judged and reflect on how you can approach these feelings with compassion. Use affirmations such as, "I am enough as I am," or "It's okay to be imperfect."

3. Exposure Therapy

Gradual exposure to feared situations can help desensitize individuals to judgment. Start small: if speaking in front of a group is intimidating, practice by sharing your thoughts with a trusted friend or family member. Gradually increase the level of exposure by participating in group discussions or joining clubs where sharing is encouraged. Each successful experience will build confidence and reduce anxiety.

4. Mindfulness and Grounding Techniques

Mindfulness can be a powerful tool for managing fear and anxiety. Engaging in mindfulness practices helps individuals remain present, reducing the tendency to ruminate on potential judgments. Techniques such as deep breathing, meditation, or grounding exercises can help anchor your thoughts in the present moment. For instance, when you notice fear creeping in, pause to take deep breaths, focusing on the sensations in your body and the environment around you.

5. Reframe Perceptions of Judgment

Instead of viewing judgment as a negative experience, try to see it as an opportunity for growth. Recognize that feedback can be valuable and that not all judgments are harmful. When faced with criticism, ask yourself if there's something constructive to learn from the situation. This shift in perspective can help lessen the emotional weight of judgment.

6. Build a Support System

Surrounding yourself with supportive individuals can provide a buffer against the fear of judgment. Share your experiences and fears with trusted friends or family members. Their encouragement can help you feel less alone and provide reassurance during challenging moments. Consider seeking out groups or communities that foster acceptance and understanding.

The Importance of Taking Action

Overcoming the fear of judgment is a journey that requires patience and persistence. It's essential to acknowledge that setbacks may occur, and that's perfectly normal. What matters most is the commitment to take action and challenge those fears. Start small, celebrate victories, and practice self-compassion along the way.

Conclusion

The fear of judgment can be a formidable barrier to living an authentic life, but it doesn't have to define your experiences. By understanding its roots, recognizing its impact, and implementing effective strategies, individuals can reclaim their confidence and find freedom in self-expression. Remember, everyone experiences judgment at some point; it's part of being human. What matters is how you respond to it. Embrace the journey of self-discovery, and know that overcoming this fear is not only possible but also profoundly liberating.

Resources for Further Support

If you find that the fear of judgment is significantly impacting your daily life, consider reaching out to a mental health professional. Therapy can provide valuable insights, coping strategies, and support tailored to your unique experiences. Additionally, self-help books and online resources focused on anxiety management, self-compassion, and mindfulness can serve as excellent tools in your journey toward overcoming fear.

Chapter 6: Time Management and Reducing Overwhelm

Prioritization and Time Blocking for Balance

Navigating the world as a teenager can often feel like juggling a million things at once. School, extracurricular activities, part-time jobs, social obligations, and family responsibilities can quickly create a sense of overwhelm. For many young adults, managing time effectively is not just a skill but a vital lifeline to maintaining mental health and emotional well-being. In this chapter, we will explore the concepts of prioritization and time blocking, two powerful techniques that can help you regain control over your schedule and reduce feelings of anxiety and stress.

The Importance of Time Management

Time management is more than just planning your day; it's about making conscious choices that reflect your values and priorities. Poor time management can lead to chronic stress, missed deadlines, and feelings of inadequacy, while effective time management fosters a sense of accomplishment and clarity. Here are several reasons why managing your time wisely is essential:

1. **Reduces Anxiety:** When you know what you need to accomplish and when, it alleviates the stress that comes from uncertainty and last-minute rushes.
2. **Enhances Productivity:** Effective time management allows you to focus on tasks that matter most, reducing procrastination and improving overall productivity.
3. **Fosters Work-Life Balance:** By setting boundaries around your time, you can ensure you make space for both responsibilities and leisure, leading to a healthier, more fulfilling life.
4. **Increases Self-Discipline:** When you commit to a structured schedule, you build self-discipline and resilience, qualities that will serve you well in all aspects of life.
5. **Promotes Personal Growth:** Allocating time for self-care, hobbies, and personal interests contributes to your overall happiness and mental health.

Understanding Prioritization

At its core, prioritization involves determining what is most important and urgent in your life. This skill allows you to allocate your time effectively and ensures that critical tasks receive the attention they need. Here's how to prioritize your tasks effectively:

1. **Identify Your Goals:** Start by reflecting on what you want to achieve in both the short term and the long term. Are your goals academic, personal, or related to your social life? Write them down, as this will give you clarity about where to focus your energy.
2. **Make a Task List:** Create a comprehensive list of everything you need to do, from daily responsibilities like homework and chores to longer-term projects like college applications or personal hobbies. Don't worry about the order just yet; the aim is to capture all tasks.
3. **Use the Eisenhower Matrix:** This tool can help you categorize tasks based on urgency and importance. The matrix consists of four quadrants:
    - **Urgent and Important:** Tasks you must do immediately.
    - **Important but Not Urgent:** Tasks that require planning and should be scheduled.
    - **Urgent but Not Important:** Tasks that can often be delegated or minimized.
    - **Neither Urgent nor Important:** Tasks that may be distractions and can often be eliminated.
4. Visualizing your tasks in this way can clarify what requires your immediate attention and what can wait.
5. **Set Deadlines:** Assign deadlines to each task, keeping in mind how long it realistically takes to complete them. This practice helps create a sense of urgency and accountability.
6. **Review and Adjust:** Priorities can change. Regularly review your task list and adjust as necessary to reflect new obligations or shifting goals.

Introduction to Time Blocking

Time blocking is a powerful technique that involves dividing your day into specific blocks of time, each dedicated to a particular task or type of work. This method not only encourages focus but also allows you to anticipate your day, making it feel less chaotic. Here's how to implement time blocking effectively:

1. **Create a Weekly Overview:** Begin by mapping out your week. This includes school hours, work shifts, and fixed commitments. Use a planner or digital calendar to visualize your schedule.
2. **Allocate Time Blocks:** Based on your task list and priorities, allocate blocks of time for different activities. For example:
    - **Morning Blocks:** Focus on schoolwork or homework.
    - **Afternoon Blocks:** Reserve time for extracurricular activities or part-time work.
    - **Evening Blocks:** Dedicate time for relaxation, hobbies, or socializing.
3. **Include Breaks:** Remember to incorporate short breaks within your blocks. Research shows that taking breaks can improve productivity and focus. Even a five-minute break to stretch or hydrate can refresh your mind.
4. **Limit Distractions:** When you enter a time block, aim to minimize distractions. This might mean turning off notifications on your phone or using apps that block distracting

websites. Inform those around you that you're in a focused work period to minimize interruptions.

5. **Stay Flexible:** Life is unpredictable. If something comes up that disrupts your schedule, adapt and adjust your time blocks as necessary. Flexibility is key to managing stress while staying productive.

Overcoming Common Challenges

Implementing prioritization and time blocking isn't always straightforward, and you may encounter challenges along the way. Here are some common hurdles and strategies to overcome them:

1. **Procrastination:** If you find yourself delaying tasks, start with small, manageable portions of work. Break large projects into smaller tasks, and use the Pomodoro Technique—work for 25 minutes and take a 5-minute break—to maintain focus.
2. **Overcommitting:** It's easy to feel pressured to say yes to every invitation or request. Learn to say no when your plate is already full. Remember that it's okay to prioritize your well-being over obligations.
3. **Feeling Overwhelmed:** If a task feels daunting, remember to break it down into smaller steps. Focus on completing one step at a time, rather than the entire project. This approach can make even the largest tasks feel manageable.
4. **Lack of Motivation:** Sometimes, the thought of a task can feel uninspiring. Find ways to make it enjoyable—listen to music, study with friends, or reward yourself with a treat after completing a difficult task.
5. **Inconsistency:** Establishing a new routine can take time. Commit to practicing prioritization and time blocking consistently for at least a few weeks. This will help these techniques become ingrained habits.

Balancing Responsibilities and Self-Care

While managing your time is crucial, it's equally important to balance responsibilities with self-care. Overloading yourself with tasks can lead to burnout, and neglecting your mental health can counteract the benefits of time management. Here are a few tips for maintaining this balance:

1. **Schedule Self-Care:** Just as you would schedule classes or work shifts, allocate time for self-care activities such as exercise, hobbies, and relaxation. These moments are essential for recharging and maintaining a healthy mindset.
2. **Incorporate Leisure into Your Blocks:** Make sure your schedule includes downtime for socializing, pursuing interests, or simply resting. Engaging in enjoyable activities can boost your mood and increase your overall productivity.

3. **Practice Mindfulness During Breaks:** Use breaks not just as a time to rest but as an opportunity to practice mindfulness. A few minutes of deep breathing or a short walk can clear your mind and refresh your focus.
4. **Evaluate Your Load:** Periodically reflect on your commitments. If you find that your schedule feels too packed, consider scaling back on certain activities or responsibilities. Quality over quantity is key to maintaining balance.

Learning to prioritize and manage your time effectively is not just a skill for today; it's a lifelong tool that will serve you well in future academic and professional endeavors. By mastering these techniques, you can cultivate a greater sense of control over your life, reduce feelings of overwhelm, and create a balanced lifestyle that accommodates both responsibilities and personal interests.

As you embark on this journey of time management, remember that it's perfectly normal to feel a little overwhelmed at first. Embrace the process, and be patient with yourself. Over time, these strategies will become second nature, empowering you to navigate the complexities of life with confidence and resilience. You have the ability to shape your time, reduce stress, and ultimately thrive in your teenage years and beyond.

Setting SMART Goals

As a mental health professional, I understand that setting goals is a fundamental aspect of personal development and mental well-being. It's not just about having a destination in mind; it's about creating a pathway that transforms dreams into achievable realities. One of the most effective frameworks for goal setting is the SMART criteria. SMART goals are Specific, Measurable, Achievable, Relevant, and Time-bound. This method provides a structured approach that helps individuals articulate their aspirations clearly and systematically.

Why SMART Goals Matter

Many of us struggle with vague intentions, like "I want to be happier" or "I need to get fit." While these statements express a desire for change, they lack clarity and direction. This can lead to feelings of frustration and discouragement when progress isn't evident. SMART goals, however, provide a solid framework for breaking down your aspirations into manageable steps, enhancing both motivation and accountability.

1. **Specific**: A specific goal addresses the 'what,' 'why,' and 'how' of your objective. It answers questions such as:
   o What do I want to achieve?
   o Why is this goal important to me?
   o How will I accomplish it?

2. For example, instead of saying, "I want to exercise more," a specific goal would be, "I want to exercise for at least 30 minutes, five days a week to improve my overall fitness and energy levels."

3. **Measurable**: Measurable goals allow you to track your progress and determine when you have reached your objective. This involves establishing concrete criteria for measurement. Consider:
    - How will I measure my progress?
    - What indicators will show that I'm moving in the right direction?

4. Continuing with our fitness example, you might say, "I will track my workouts in a journal or fitness app to ensure I complete at least 150 minutes of exercise each week."

5. **Achievable**: While it's essential to aim high, your goals should also be realistic and attainable. This means considering your current circumstances and resources. Reflect on:
    - Is this goal realistic given my current situation?
    - What steps do I need to take to achieve this?

6. For instance, if you currently don't exercise at all, aiming to run a marathon next month may not be achievable. A more realistic goal might be, "I will start by walking for 15 minutes every day, gradually increasing the duration and intensity."

7. **Relevant**: Goals should align with your broader life objectives and values. This relevance ensures that your efforts contribute meaningfully to your overall life satisfaction. Ask yourself:
    - Does this goal matter to me?
    - How does it fit into my larger aspirations?

8. If you want to improve your physical health, then a goal to "join a local gym and attend three classes each week" is relevant and supports your health objectives.

9. **Time-bound**: Setting a deadline creates a sense of urgency and prompts action. It encourages you to prioritize your goal amid life's distractions. Consider:
    - What is my deadline for this goal?
    - How will I hold myself accountable?

10. A time-bound version of our fitness goal could be, "I will achieve this by the end of the next three months, reassessing my progress at the end of each month."

Crafting Your SMART Goals

Now that you understand the components of SMART goals, it's time to craft your own. Here's a step-by-step approach:

1. **Reflect on Your Aspirations**: Begin by taking some time to think about what you truly want to achieve. This could be in various areas of your life, such as health, relationships, education, or personal development.

2. **Write Down Your Goals**: Documenting your thoughts helps solidify them. Start with a broad goal and then refine it using the SMART criteria.

3. **Break Down the Goals**: Larger goals can often feel overwhelming. Break them down into smaller, actionable steps. This not only makes them more manageable but also provides opportunities for celebrating small victories along the way.
4. **Create an Action Plan**: Outline specific actions you will take to achieve each step. This might include scheduling time in your calendar, seeking resources, or connecting with accountability partners.
5. **Review and Adjust**: Life is unpredictable. Regularly review your progress and be open to adjusting your goals as needed. If you find that a goal no longer feels relevant or achievable, it's okay to modify it.

Overcoming Challenges in Goal Setting

Setting SMART goals is a powerful strategy, but challenges may arise along the way. Here are some common hurdles and strategies to overcome them:

1. **Fear of Failure**: It's natural to feel apprehensive about failing. Reframe your mindset by viewing setbacks as opportunities for growth and learning. Remember, progress isn't linear; every step, even backward ones, contributes to your overall journey.
2. **Lack of Motivation**: Motivation can wane over time. To combat this, regularly remind yourself of your 'why'—the underlying reasons for pursuing your goal. Keep a visual reminder of your goal or find a supportive community that shares similar aspirations.
3. **Perfectionism**: The desire to do everything perfectly can paralyze you from taking action. Embrace the concept of "good enough." Focus on progress rather than perfection, and celebrate the effort you put into moving forward.
4. **Time Management**: Balancing multiple responsibilities can make it challenging to prioritize your goals. Use time-blocking techniques to allocate specific time slots for working on your goals, ensuring you carve out space in your busy life.

The Role of Accountability

Accountability can significantly enhance your commitment to achieving your SMART goals. Consider finding an accountability partner—someone who supports your journey and checks in with you regularly. This could be a friend, family member, or even a mentor. Sharing your goals with someone else can create a sense of obligation and encouragement.

Setting SMART goals is an empowering process that can transform your aspirations into achievable realities. By making your goals specific, measurable, achievable, relevant, and time-bound, you create a clear roadmap to follow. Remember that the journey toward achieving your goals may have ups and downs, and that's perfectly okay. Each step you take is a step toward growth, resilience, and personal fulfillment.

As you embark on your goal-setting journey, keep in mind that it's not just about reaching the destination; it's also about enjoying the process, learning about yourself, and building skills that will serve you for a lifetime. So grab a notebook, start reflecting, and let the power of SMART goals guide you toward a more focused and fulfilling life.

Managing Screen Time and Digital Detox

In an increasingly digital world, screens have become an integral part of our lives. They connect us to friends and family, provide entertainment, and serve as portals to information. However, excessive screen time can negatively impact mental health, particularly among teenagers. Managing screen time and engaging in a digital detox are crucial for fostering healthier habits and enhancing overall well-being. In this chapter, we'll explore the psychological implications of excessive screen use, the importance of mindfulness in managing screen time, and practical strategies for conducting a digital detox.

Understanding the Impact of Screen Time on Mental Health

The allure of screens is undeniable; they are designed to capture our attention. Social media platforms, gaming, streaming services, and endless content offer instant gratification. Yet, this constant stimulation can lead to various mental health issues, including anxiety, depression, and reduced attention spans. The World Health Organization suggests that excessive screen time can lead to sleep disturbances, mood swings, and increased feelings of isolation.

1. **Anxiety and Depression:** Studies have found a correlation between high screen time and increased rates of anxiety and depression. Social media can create a false sense of reality, where constant comparisons with others lead to feelings of inadequacy and low self-esteem. This cycle of comparison can escalate into a persistent fear of missing out (FOMO), causing heightened anxiety.
2. **Sleep Disruption:** Engaging with screens, especially before bed, can disrupt sleep patterns. The blue light emitted by screens interferes with the production of melatonin, the hormone responsible for regulating sleep. Poor sleep quality can further exacerbate anxiety and depression, leading to a vicious cycle of mental health struggles.
3. **Reduced Attention Span:** Continuous exposure to fast-paced media can condition our brains to expect instant rewards, leading to decreased attention spans. This can affect academic performance, relationships, and overall cognitive functioning.
4. **Isolation and Loneliness:** Paradoxically, while screens connect us virtually, excessive use can lead to feelings of isolation. Engaging in real-life interactions becomes more challenging when we are preoccupied with digital distractions. The more we immerse ourselves in our screens, the more we may withdraw from face-to-face connections, exacerbating feelings of loneliness.

The Role of Mindfulness in Managing Screen Time

Mindfulness, the practice of being fully present and engaged in the moment without judgment, can play a significant role in managing screen time. By incorporating mindfulness techniques, teens can develop a healthier relationship with technology. Here are several mindfulness strategies to help reduce screen time and promote mental well-being:

1. **Mindful Awareness:** Begin by observing your screen habits without judgment. Track how much time you spend on various platforms and note the feelings and thoughts that arise during and after usage. This practice of self-awareness can help you identify triggers that lead to excessive screen time.
2. **Setting Intentions:** Before engaging with your device, set a clear intention. Ask yourself: "What do I hope to achieve by using my phone or computer?" Whether it's connecting with friends, learning something new, or simply relaxing, having a clear purpose can help you use your devices more intentionally.
3. **Digital Journaling:** Maintain a digital journal to record your screen time habits, thoughts, and emotions related to technology use. Reflecting on these entries can help you identify patterns, triggers, and the impact of screen time on your mood and well-being.
4. **Mindful Breaks:** Integrate short mindful breaks into your day. Step away from your screen, take a few deep breaths, and engage in activities that ground you, such as stretching, walking, or practicing gratitude. These breaks can help reset your mind and reduce the urge to reach for your device constantly.

Practical Strategies for a Digital Detox

A digital detox is an intentional period during which you abstain from or significantly reduce your screen time to promote mental well-being. Here are actionable steps to conduct a successful digital detox:

1. **Establish Boundaries:** Define specific timeframes for screen use. Consider implementing screen-free zones, such as the dinner table or the bedroom, to encourage more meaningful interactions and promote better sleep.
2. **Create a Schedule:** Develop a weekly plan that outlines your screen time. Allocate specific times for social media, gaming, and recreational browsing, while ensuring that ample time is reserved for offline activities, hobbies, and social interactions.
3. **Declutter Your Digital Space:** Unsubscribe from unnecessary notifications, delete unused apps, and curate your social media feeds. This will not only reduce distractions but also create a more positive digital environment.
4. **Engage in Offline Activities:** Replace screen time with activities that promote well-being. Explore new hobbies, engage in physical exercise, read books, or spend time

outdoors. These activities can provide a fulfilling alternative to screen time and improve your mood.

5. **Connect with Nature:** Nature has a calming effect on the mind. Dedicate time to disconnect from screens and immerse yourself in nature. Whether it's a walk in the park, hiking, or simply sitting outside, this connection can enhance your overall well-being.

6. **Find Support:** Involve friends and family in your digital detox journey. Share your goals with them and encourage each other to stick to your plans. Having a support system can motivate you and make the process more enjoyable.

7. **Evaluate Your Progress:** After a week or month of digital detox, take time to reflect on your experience. What did you learn about yourself? How did it affect your mood and relationships? Use this evaluation to adjust your screen time habits moving forward.

8. **Set Long-Term Goals:** Rather than viewing the digital detox as a temporary fix, consider making it a lifestyle change. Set long-term goals for maintaining a healthy balance between screen time and offline activities. This could include regular screen-free weekends, digital-free days, or planned tech-free vacations.

Managing screen time and engaging in a digital detox is essential for promoting mental well-being among teenagers. The potential adverse effects of excessive screen use—such as anxiety, depression, and sleep disruption—highlight the need for mindfulness and intentionality in our digital habits. By implementing practical strategies, we can foster healthier relationships with technology, enhance our mental health, and cultivate a more balanced life. Remember, it's not about eliminating screens entirely but about finding a harmonious balance that allows for both connection and personal well-being. Taking control of your screen time is a significant step towards nurturing a healthier, more fulfilling life.

Chapter 7: Grounding Techniques and Stress Relief

The 5-4-3-2-1 Grounding Technique

In today's fast-paced world, where the pressures of school, social interactions, and future uncertainties weigh heavily on young minds, it's no wonder that anxiety and overthinking have become pervasive challenges for teenagers. Amidst this chaos, grounding techniques can serve as powerful tools for reclaiming a sense of calm and control. In this chapter, we will delve deep into grounding techniques, focusing particularly on the **5-4-3-2-1 Grounding Technique**—a simple yet effective method that can help anchor your thoughts and emotions in the present moment.

Understanding Grounding Techniques

Before we dive into the specifics of the 5-4-3-2-1 technique, it's crucial to understand what grounding techniques are and how they can benefit you. Grounding techniques are strategies designed to help individuals connect with the present moment and distract themselves from overwhelming emotions or thoughts. They are particularly useful during times of anxiety, panic, or stress, as they can bring your focus back to reality and away from spiraling thoughts.

The beauty of grounding techniques lies in their versatility; they can be used anywhere, anytime, and require no special equipment or training. Grounding not only helps in reducing anxiety but also aids in enhancing emotional regulation and mindfulness. By anchoring yourself to the present, you can develop a greater awareness of your surroundings and a sense of safety within your own body.

Introducing the 5-4-3-2-1 Grounding Technique

The **5-4-3-2-1 Grounding Technique** is a sensory-based exercise that guides you to notice your environment through your five senses. It's a straightforward process, but it can be transformative, especially when you feel overwhelmed. This technique can be performed in a matter of minutes and can be done in virtually any setting—at school, home, or even during a walk in the park.

How to Use the 5-4-3-2-1 Technique

1. **Find a Comfortable Position**: Begin by sitting or standing in a comfortable position. Take a moment to breathe deeply, inhaling through your nose and exhaling through your mouth. Allow yourself to feel the weight of your body on the chair or the ground.
2. **Engage Your Senses**:

- 5 **Things You Can See**: Look around you and notice five things that you can see. It could be the pattern on the wall, the color of your shirt, or the way the light reflects off a surface. Describe them in your mind or out loud. For example, you might say, "I see a blue notebook, a plant in the corner, a poster of my favorite band, a clock on the wall, and a pen on the table." Focusing on visual details can help shift your attention away from anxious thoughts.

- 4 **Things You Can Touch**: Now, focus on four things you can feel. This can include the texture of your clothes, the feeling of the chair beneath you, the ground under your feet, or even the sensation of your hands resting on your lap. Engage with the texture and temperature of each item. For instance, you might think, "I feel the smooth fabric of my shirt, the hard surface of the chair, the coolness of the air on my skin, and the warmth of my hands."

- 3 **Things You Can Hear**: Next, listen closely for three sounds in your environment. This might be the rustling of leaves, distant chatter, or the hum of an air conditioner. Acknowledge each sound and try to describe them: "I hear the sound of my breathing, the faint music playing from a nearby classroom, and the tapping of someone typing on a keyboard." This step encourages you to become more aware of your surroundings and the present moment.

- 2 **Things You Can Smell**: Now, notice two smells in your environment. If you can't identify specific smells, think of your favorite scents. Perhaps it's the aroma of fresh coffee, the smell of rain, or a hint of perfume. If you're unable to identify any scents in the moment, simply recall two scents you enjoy, like the smell of fresh cookies or a floral fragrance.

- 1 **Thing You Can Taste**: Finally, focus on one thing you can taste. This could be the lingering taste of a snack you had earlier, a sip of water, or even the sensation of your tongue against your teeth. If there's nothing currently in your mouth, consider what your favorite flavor is—maybe chocolate, strawberries, or mint.

3. **Take a Moment to Reflect**: Once you've gone through the 5-4-3-2-1 process, take a moment to reflect on your experience. Notice how you feel compared to when you started. Are you more centered? Did your anxiety lessen? This brief pause allows you to integrate the calming effects of the exercise.

The Science Behind Grounding Techniques

Understanding the neuroscience behind grounding techniques can help reinforce their importance in managing anxiety. When you engage your senses, you shift your focus from the amygdala—the part of your brain responsible for the fight-or-flight response—toward the prefrontal cortex, which is responsible for reasoning and decision-making. This shift can help reduce the intensity of your anxious feelings and provide clarity in a moment of chaos.

Moreover, grounding techniques like the 5-4-3-2-1 exercise foster mindfulness, encouraging you to live in the present rather than ruminating about the past or worrying about the future. Mindfulness has been shown to reduce stress, improve emotional regulation, and enhance overall mental well-being, making it a powerful practice for teenagers navigating the complexities of life.

Integrating Grounding Techniques into Daily Life

To maximize the benefits of grounding techniques, it's essential to integrate them into your daily routine. Here are some tips for incorporating the 5-4-3-2-1 technique into your life:

1. **Practice Regularly**: Set aside time each day to practice the 5-4-3-2-1 technique, even when you're not feeling anxious. Regular practice can help you become more familiar with the exercise, making it easier to implement when stress arises.
2. **Use Reminders**: Create visual reminders, such as sticky notes on your mirror or phone, to prompt you to practice grounding techniques throughout your day.
3. **Pair with Other Techniques**: Consider combining the 5-4-3-2-1 exercise with other mindfulness practices, such as meditation, yoga, or deep breathing exercises, to enhance your overall sense of calm.
4. **Share with Friends**: Discuss grounding techniques with your friends or family members. Practicing together can reinforce your commitment and create a support system for managing anxiety.
5. **Customize the Technique**: Feel free to adapt the 5-4-3-2-1 technique to fit your preferences. For instance, if you find certain senses more calming than others, focus on those. The key is to find what works best for you.

Grounding techniques, particularly the 5-4-3-2-1 method, offer teenagers a practical and effective way to manage anxiety and overthinking. By engaging your senses and reconnecting with the present moment, you can gain clarity, reduce stress, and cultivate resilience in the face of life's challenges. Remember, it's perfectly normal to feel overwhelmed at times, but with the right tools and techniques, you can navigate these feelings and emerge stronger. Embrace the practice of grounding, and allow it to empower you on your journey toward mental well-being.

Progressive Muscle Relaxation

In our fast-paced world, stress has become an all-too-common companion, often manifesting in physical tension that can exacerbate our mental and emotional challenges. One effective technique to combat this tension is **Progressive Muscle Relaxation (PMR)**, a method developed by Dr. Edmund Jacobson in the early 20th century. PMR focuses on systematically tensing and then relaxing different muscle groups in the body, promoting a deep state of relaxation. This guide will explore the theory behind PMR, how to practice it effectively, and the myriad benefits it can provide.

The Science Behind PMR

At its core, PMR is rooted in the understanding of the mind-body connection. When we experience stress, our bodies respond with a "fight or flight" reaction, which includes muscle tension. Over time, chronic stress can lead to sustained tension, contributing to physical ailments like headaches, back pain, and digestive issues. PMR works by disrupting this cycle. By consciously tensing and relaxing muscles, we create a heightened awareness of our physical sensations and promote a state of calm.

When you tense a muscle, you increase blood flow to that area, providing oxygen and nutrients. When you release that tension, the blood flow decreases, allowing the muscles to relax completely. This contrast helps your body and mind distinguish between tension and relaxation, which can be particularly beneficial for individuals who may not be aware of their physical stress.

How PMR Works: Step-by-Step

Preparation for PMR:

1. **Find a Comfortable Space:** Choose a quiet, comfortable environment where you won't be disturbed. This could be a cozy corner of your home, a quiet park, or even your car if you need a quick break.
2. **Get Comfortable:** Sit or lie down in a position that feels comfortable. Make sure your clothes aren't too tight, as this can distract you from the relaxation process.
3. **Set Your Intention:** Take a moment to set an intention for your practice. This might be to relieve stress, reduce anxiety, or simply to reconnect with your body.

The PMR Technique:

1. **Take Deep Breaths:** Start by taking a few deep breaths. Inhale slowly through your nose, allowing your abdomen to expand. Hold for a moment, then exhale through your mouth. Repeat this three to five times, focusing on the sensation of your breath.
2. **Focus on Your Feet:** Begin with your feet. Tense the muscles in your feet as tightly as you can for about five seconds. Feel the tension build. Then, suddenly release the tension and notice the difference between tension and relaxation. Spend a few moments enjoying the feeling of relaxation.
3. **Move Upward Through Your Body:** Continue this process, working your way up through your body:
   - **Calves:** Tense for five seconds, then release.

- ○ **Thighs:** Tense, hold, and release.
- ○ **Buttocks:** Tense tightly, hold, and let go.
- ○ **Stomach:** Suck in your stomach as much as possible, hold, and release.
- ○ **Back:** Arch your back gently, hold the tension, and relax.
- ○ **Hands:** Make fists, hold for five seconds, and then release.
- ○ **Arms:** Tense your arms by bending them at the elbows, hold, and relax.
- ○ **Shoulders:** Lift your shoulders up towards your ears, hold, and let them drop.
- ○ **Face:** Tense all the muscles in your face (squeeze your eyes shut, clench your jaw), hold, and release.

4. **Complete the Session:** After you have worked through all the muscle groups, take a few moments to lie quietly, enjoying the feeling of relaxation throughout your body. Focus on your breathing and allow any remaining tension to dissolve.

Tips for Effective PMR Practice

- **Practice Regularly:** The more frequently you practice PMR, the more effective it will be. Aim for at least once a day, or whenever you feel stress creeping in.
- **Be Patient:** It may take time to feel the full benefits of PMR. If you find it difficult to relax at first, don't get discouraged. Keep practicing.
- **Combine with Other Techniques:** PMR can be enhanced by combining it with deep breathing, guided imagery, or mindfulness meditation. Consider listening to soothing music or a relaxation app to enhance your experience.
- **Stay Mindful:** As you practice PMR, remain mindful of your body's sensations. Notice where you hold tension and how it feels to release it.

Benefits of Progressive Muscle Relaxation

The benefits of PMR extend beyond immediate relaxation. Here are some of the most significant advantages:

1. **Reduced Anxiety and Stress:** PMR helps lower cortisol levels, reducing overall feelings of anxiety and stress. Many individuals find that regular practice leads to improved emotional regulation.
2. **Improved Sleep Quality:** By promoting physical relaxation, PMR can help individuals fall asleep more easily and achieve deeper sleep. This is particularly beneficial for those who experience insomnia or racing thoughts at night.
3. **Enhanced Focus and Concentration:** By training your body to recognize and release tension, PMR can help clear your mind, improving focus and cognitive performance.
4. **Increased Body Awareness:** PMR cultivates a heightened sense of awareness regarding where you hold tension in your body. This can lead to better self-care practices and lifestyle adjustments.

5. **Pain Relief:** Some studies suggest that PMR may help alleviate chronic pain by promoting relaxation and reducing muscle tension.
6. **Enhanced Coping Skills:** Regular practice can equip individuals with tools to manage stress more effectively, contributing to greater resilience in the face of challenges.

PMR in Daily Life

Integrating PMR into your daily routine doesn't have to be time-consuming. Here are a few ways to incorporate this technique into your life:

- **Morning Routine:** Start your day with a quick PMR session to set a calm tone for the day ahead.
- **Midday Break:** Take a few minutes during your lunch break to practice PMR, especially if you find work stressful.
- **Evening Wind-Down:** Use PMR as part of your evening routine to help your mind and body transition into a restful state.
- **Before Important Events:** If you have a big presentation or exam, practicing PMR beforehand can help reduce nerves and improve performance.

Progressive Muscle Relaxation is a powerful tool that can lead to significant improvements in your mental and physical well-being. By investing time in this practice, you cultivate a greater sense of control over your body and mind, allowing you to navigate life's stresses with increased resilience. Whether you're a teenager facing the pressures of school or an adult juggling multiple responsibilities, PMR can serve as a reliable anchor in your journey toward stress management and emotional balance. Remember, the key to mastering PMR lies in consistent practice and an open mind—embrace the process, and enjoy the journey toward relaxation and peace.

Using Visualization and Guided Imagery

In today's fast-paced world, where the pressures of life can often feel overwhelming, many teenagers find themselves grappling with anxiety and the pervasive habit of overthinking. One powerful and effective technique that can provide relief is **visualization** and **guided imagery**. These practices not only foster relaxation but also empower young minds to navigate their thoughts and emotions more effectively. Let's delve into what these techniques entail, how they work, and how you can incorporate them into your daily routine.

Understanding Visualization and Guided Imagery

Visualization involves creating vivid mental images to influence your emotional and physical state. It's the process of imagining a scenario in detail, which can help your brain perceive it as a real experience. For example, if you visualize yourself confidently speaking in front of a crowd, your brain begins to create neural pathways associated with that successful experience, making it easier to replicate in reality.

Guided imagery, on the other hand, is a more structured practice where a facilitator (often a therapist or a recorded guide) leads you through a series of imagery exercises. This can involve various sensory experiences, including sounds, colors, and textures, designed to evoke feelings of peace, safety, and relaxation.

Both techniques draw from the same psychological principles but differ in execution. They are powerful tools for managing anxiety, reducing stress, and fostering a positive mindset.

The Science Behind Visualization

The effectiveness of visualization can be traced back to its impact on the brain. Neuroscientific research has shown that the same brain regions activated during actual experiences are also engaged during imagined scenarios. This means that when you visualize achieving a goal or overcoming a challenge, your brain processes that experience similarly to how it would if it were happening in real life.

For teenagers struggling with anxiety, visualization can serve as a rehearsal tool. Whether it's preparing for a test, a sports competition, or a social event, visualizing success can help mitigate fear and build confidence. Research has also demonstrated that athletes who engage in visualization practices often see improved performance outcomes, a principle that can be applied across various domains of life.

How Visualization and Guided Imagery Help with Overthinking

1. Reducing Anxiety
Overthinking often leads to heightened anxiety. Visualization provides a mental escape by allowing individuals to focus on positive outcomes instead of potential negative scenarios. By creating a mental sanctuary—whether it's a serene beach or a cozy forest—teens can reduce the intensity of their anxious thoughts and create a calming mental space.

2. Enhancing Emotional Regulation
Visualization helps young adults develop emotional awareness and regulation. When they practice visualizing specific situations that provoke anxiety (like giving a presentation), they can confront their fears in a safe and controlled manner. This practice helps them learn how to manage their emotions effectively in real-life scenarios.

3. Promoting Relaxation and Mindfulness
Guided imagery sessions often incorporate relaxation techniques, such as deep breathing and progressive muscle relaxation. These practices can significantly decrease physiological

symptoms of stress, such as a racing heart and tense muscles, leading to a more profound sense of peace.

4. Building Resilience

The more a teen engages with visualization, the more resilient they become. They learn to face challenges with a positive mindset, making them less likely to succumb to negative thought patterns. This resilience can lead to improved self-esteem and confidence, enabling them to tackle obstacles head-on.

How to Practice Visualization and Guided Imagery

1. Finding a Quiet Space

To start your visualization practice, find a comfortable and quiet space where you can sit or lie down without distractions. This could be your bedroom, a park, or any place where you feel at ease.

2. Setting an Intention

Before you begin, set a clear intention for your visualization. This could be a specific goal (e.g., feeling calm before an exam) or a general desire for relaxation. Having a clear focus will enhance the effectiveness of your practice.

3. Using Deep Breathing

Begin with a few minutes of deep breathing. Inhale deeply through your nose, allowing your abdomen to expand, and then exhale slowly through your mouth. Repeat this several times, allowing your body to relax with each breath.

4. Engaging the Senses

As you start to visualize, engage all your senses. If you are imagining a peaceful beach, picture the golden sand under your feet, hear the gentle waves lapping at the shore, and feel the warmth of the sun on your skin. The more detailed and vivid your imagery, the more effective it will be.

5. Incorporating Guided Imagery

If you prefer guided imagery, you can use recorded scripts or apps that lead you through visualization exercises. Look for resources specifically designed for teens, which can provide relatable scenarios and calming narratives.

6. Practicing Regularly

Like any skill, visualization requires practice. Aim to incorporate it into your daily routine, whether that's for five minutes in the morning, during a lunch break, or before bed. Consistent practice will strengthen your ability to visualize effectively.

7. Journaling Your Experiences

After each visualization session, take a few moments to journal about your experience. What images came to mind? How did you feel? Writing about your experiences can reinforce the positive outcomes of visualization and help track your progress over time.

Example Visualization Exercise

Here's a simple visualization exercise you can try:

The Safe Place Visualization

1. **Find a Comfortable Position**: Sit or lie down in a quiet space. Close your eyes and take a few deep breaths.
2. **Create Your Safe Place**: Imagine a place where you feel completely safe and relaxed. This could be a real location, like your favorite vacation spot, or a fictional one, like a magical forest.
3. **Engage Your Senses**: Begin to explore this place in your mind. What do you see? Notice the colors and shapes around you. What sounds do you hear? Maybe the rustling of leaves or the sound of water flowing. What scents are in the air? Perhaps the smell of flowers or fresh pine.
4. **Feel the Environment**: Imagine the sensation of being in this place. Feel the ground beneath your feet, the gentle breeze against your skin, or the warmth of the sun.
5. **Allow Yourself to Relax**: As you immerse yourself in this visualization, allow your body to relax further with each breath. If any anxious thoughts arise, acknowledge them and let them drift away like clouds in the sky.
6. **Stay as Long as You Need**: Spend a few minutes in your safe place, enjoying the peace it brings you. When you feel ready, gradually bring your awareness back to the present moment, wiggle your fingers and toes, and slowly open your eyes.

Visualization and guided imagery are valuable tools that can significantly impact a teenager's ability to manage anxiety and overcome overthinking. By incorporating these techniques into their daily routine, teens can develop greater emotional resilience, enhance their mental well-being, and navigate life's challenges with confidence.

The beauty of these practices lies in their accessibility; they require no special equipment or extensive training, just a willingness to explore the power of the mind. As you embark on this journey, remember that it's perfectly normal to experience challenges along the way. With patience, practice, and persistence, you can harness the transformative power of visualization to create a brighter, more balanced future.

Chapter 8: Building Resilience and Letting Go of Perfectionism

How Perfectionism Fuels Anxiety

Understanding Perfectionism

Perfectionism is often perceived as a positive trait. We hear phrases like "striving for excellence" or "going above and beyond," which can make perfectionism seem admirable. However, when we dig deeper, we discover that perfectionism can become a double-edged sword. At its core, perfectionism is the relentless pursuit of flawlessness. It often leads to a vicious cycle of setting excessively high standards and then feeling inadequate when those standards aren't met.

The Psychology Behind Perfectionism

Perfectionism is deeply rooted in psychological and social factors. Many individuals develop perfectionist tendencies in childhood. Messages from parents, teachers, or peers that emphasize achievement can create a fear of failure. This fear can manifest as anxiety, leading young people to believe that their worth is tied to their accomplishments. As a result, perfectionists may constantly feel pressured to perform at an unattainable level, fostering a sense of chronic dissatisfaction.

How Perfectionism Fuels Anxiety

1. The Pressure to Succeed

The pressure to succeed can be overwhelming for perfectionists. Every task becomes a monumental challenge, as the fear of not meeting expectations looms large. This constant state of anxiety can lead to stress-related symptoms, such as insomnia, headaches, and difficulty concentrating. The belief that one must always excel can create a toxic environment where mistakes are unacceptable, further heightening anxiety levels.

2. Fear of Judgment and Criticism

Perfectionists are often preoccupied with what others think. They fear judgment and criticism, believing that if they fall short of their high standards, they will be seen as failures. This fear can be paralyzing, preventing them from taking risks or pursuing opportunities. The desire for external validation can create a cycle of anxiety, as perfectionists constantly seek approval from others while fearing their disapproval.

3. Procrastination and Avoidance

Ironically, perfectionism can lead to procrastination. When faced with a task, the overwhelming desire to produce a perfect outcome can make it difficult to start. The fear of not meeting one's own standards may result in avoidance behavior, causing the individual to delay important tasks. This procrastination often leads to increased stress as deadlines approach, creating a cycle of anxiety and self-criticism.

4. The All-or-Nothing Mindset

Perfectionists often adopt an all-or-nothing mindset, where anything less than perfect is deemed unacceptable. This black-and-white thinking can lead to feelings of failure when the outcome doesn't match the ideal. For example, a student who scores 90% on a test may focus solely on the 10% they missed, feeling like a failure rather than recognizing their achievement. This relentless self-criticism further exacerbates anxiety and erodes self-esteem.

Recognizing the Signs of Perfectionism

To combat perfectionism, it's essential to recognize its signs. Individuals may find themselves:

- **Setting unrealistically high standards**: Constantly striving for the best, even in minor tasks, can create unnecessary pressure.
- **Engaging in negative self-talk**: Perfectionists often criticize themselves harshly for perceived failures or shortcomings.
- **Avoiding challenges**: The fear of not being perfect can lead to avoidance of new experiences or challenges, limiting personal growth.
- **Feeling overwhelmed by tasks**: The inability to meet high standards can result in a sense of being overwhelmed, making it difficult to take action.

Building Resilience Through Self-Compassion

To move away from perfectionism, cultivating resilience through self-compassion is crucial. Self-compassion involves treating oneself with kindness and understanding during difficult times. Here are several strategies to foster self-compassion:

1. Practice Mindful Awareness

Mindfulness allows individuals to observe their thoughts without judgment. By practicing mindfulness, perfectionists can become more aware of their perfectionistic tendencies and the anxiety that accompanies them. This awareness is the first step toward change, enabling them to challenge these thoughts and replace them with more balanced perspectives.

2. Embrace Imperfection

Accepting that imperfection is part of the human experience is vital. Encourage yourself to take risks and embrace the possibility of failure. Remember that mistakes are not a reflection of your worth; they are opportunities for growth and learning. Challenge the belief that everything must be perfect, and allow yourself to be vulnerable in pursuit of your goals.

3. Reframe Negative Self-Talk

When faced with negative thoughts, practice reframing them. Instead of thinking, "I must be perfect," consider saying, "I am doing my best, and that is enough." Replacing harsh self-criticism with more supportive language can help alleviate anxiety and promote a healthier self-image.

4. Set Realistic Goals

Instead of aiming for perfection, focus on setting realistic and achievable goals. Break larger tasks into smaller, manageable steps to reduce feelings of overwhelm. Celebrate your progress along the way, acknowledging your efforts rather than fixating on the outcome.

Strategies for Letting Go of Perfectionism

1. **Challenge Perfectionistic Beliefs**
   Reflect on the origins of your perfectionistic beliefs. Are they rooted in societal expectations, family upbringing, or personal experiences? Recognizing these influences can help you understand the unrealistic nature of your standards.
2. **Focus on the Process, Not Just the Outcome**
   Shift your attention from the final result to the process of learning and growth. Acknowledge the effort you put in, regardless of the outcome. By valuing the journey, you can foster a sense of achievement even in imperfection.
3. **Establish a Support System**
   Surround yourself with supportive friends, family, or mentors who understand your struggles with perfectionism. Sharing your thoughts and feelings can provide relief and help you realize you're not alone in your experiences.
4. **Practice Gratitude**
   Cultivating gratitude can shift your focus from what you lack to what you have. Take time each day to reflect on the positive aspects of your life, no matter how small. This practice can help reduce feelings of inadequacy and enhance overall well-being.

Building Resilience: Embracing Imperfection

Resilience is the ability to bounce back from setbacks and adapt to challenges. Building resilience is particularly important for those struggling with perfectionism. Here's how you can develop this vital skill:

1. **Develop Problem-Solving Skills**

   Resilient individuals are effective problem solvers. Practice breaking problems down into smaller parts and brainstorming solutions. This proactive approach can empower you to tackle challenges without fear of failure.

2. **Learn from Failure**

   Instead of fearing failure, view it as an opportunity for growth. Reflect on past experiences where you faced setbacks. What did you learn? How can you apply these lessons moving forward? Embracing failure as part of the learning process can help you develop resilience.

3. **Cultivate a Growth Mindset**

   Adopting a growth mindset involves believing that your abilities can be developed through dedication and hard work. This perspective fosters a love for learning and resilience in the face of challenges. Celebrate your efforts, and recognize that improvement takes time.

4. **Practice Self-Care**

   Prioritize self-care to maintain your mental and emotional well-being. Engage in activities that bring you joy and relaxation, whether it's spending time with loved ones, pursuing hobbies, or practicing mindfulness techniques. Taking care of yourself is essential for building resilience.

Letting go of perfectionism is not an overnight process; it's a journey that requires patience, self-compassion, and resilience. As you navigate this path, remember that you are not alone. Many individuals grapple with perfectionistic tendencies, and recognizing the impact of these tendencies on your mental health is the first step toward positive change.

By embracing imperfection and focusing on personal growth rather than unattainable standards, you can cultivate resilience and foster a healthier relationship with yourself. Allow yourself the grace to be human, to make mistakes, and to learn from them. In doing so, you will not only reduce anxiety but also pave the way for a more fulfilling, authentic life.

Embracing Setbacks as Learning Opportunities

Life is filled with ups and downs, triumphs and tribulations. For many teenagers, setbacks can feel like monumental failures, leading to feelings of disappointment, frustration, and self-doubt. However, what if we could shift our perspective on these challenging moments? Instead of viewing setbacks as failures, we can learn to embrace them as valuable learning opportunities. This chapter will explore how to reframe setbacks, the importance of resilience, and actionable strategies for turning adversity into growth.

Understanding Setbacks

Setbacks can occur in various forms—academic failures, rejection from friends, sports losses, or personal challenges. Each setback can feel isolating and overwhelming, often leading to negative self-talk and anxiety. It's crucial to recognize that setbacks are a natural part of life, especially during the teenage years when individuals are still discovering their identities and navigating complex social landscapes.

The Emotional Toll of Setbacks

When a setback occurs, it's normal to experience a range of emotions. You might feel sad, angry, or even ashamed. These feelings can create a cycle of negative thoughts that exacerbate the situation. A failed test, for example, might lead you to think, "I'm not smart enough," or "I'll never succeed." Such thoughts can undermine your confidence and make you more likely to avoid challenges in the future. This cycle can become a barrier to personal growth.

The Myth of Perfection

The pressure to succeed can be immense, particularly for teens who may feel the weight of expectations from parents, peers, and society. The myth of perfection—believing that we must achieve a flawless standard in everything we do—can exacerbate the pain of setbacks. It's important to recognize that perfection is unattainable, and everyone experiences failures at some point in their lives.

The Power of Perspective

Reframing Setbacks

One of the most powerful tools in overcoming setbacks is the ability to reframe our thinking. Reframing involves changing the way we perceive a situation. Instead of asking, "Why did this happen to me?" try asking, "What can I learn from this experience?" This simple shift can open the door to new insights and growth.

Consider the story of Thomas Edison, who famously said, "I have not failed. I've just found 10,000 ways that won't work." Edison's perspective on failure as a learning experience led to his groundbreaking inventions. Embracing a similar mindset can help you view setbacks not as roadblocks but as stepping stones on your journey.

Developing a Growth Mindset

Carol Dweck, a psychologist at Stanford University, introduced the concept of a "growth mindset." This mindset is characterized by the belief that abilities and intelligence can be developed through dedication and hard work. When you cultivate a growth mindset, setbacks become opportunities for growth and learning rather than evidence of inadequacy.

For example, if you don't make the basketball team, instead of thinking, "I'm just not good at sports," try thinking, "I can improve my skills with practice." This shift in mindset encourages resilience and persistence, qualities essential for overcoming obstacles.

The Importance of Resilience

What is Resilience?

Resilience is the ability to bounce back from adversity and maintain mental health in the face of challenges. It's not about avoiding difficulties; rather, it's about developing the capacity to recover from them. Resilient individuals view setbacks as temporary and manageable, which allows them to navigate life's challenges with greater ease.

Building Resilience

Resilience can be cultivated through various strategies:

1. **Develop Strong Relationships**: Surrounding yourself with supportive friends and family can provide the encouragement you need during tough times. Openly discussing your feelings with trusted individuals can alleviate stress and foster a sense of belonging.
2. **Practice Self-Compassion**: Being kind to yourself during moments of failure is essential. Instead of criticizing yourself for not meeting expectations, treat yourself with the same kindness you would offer a friend facing a similar situation.
3. **Set Realistic Goals**: Break larger goals into smaller, achievable steps. This approach helps build confidence and allows you to celebrate small victories along the way, reducing the impact of setbacks.
4. **Embrace Change**: Life is inherently unpredictable, and being adaptable can strengthen your resilience. Accept that change is a part of life and can lead to new opportunities and experiences.
5. **Focus on What You Can Control**: In times of difficulty, it's easy to become overwhelmed by factors outside your control. Focus on what you can influence—your effort, attitude, and response to challenges—rather than dwelling on external circumstances.

Learning from Setbacks

Identifying Lessons

Once you've reframed a setback, take time to identify the lessons it holds. This process can involve reflecting on the experience, journaling your thoughts, or discussing it with someone you trust. Consider these questions to guide your reflection:

- What went wrong, and why?
- What were my thoughts and feelings during this experience?
- How did I respond to the setback?
- What would I do differently next time?
- What skills or knowledge did I gain from this experience?

By examining these questions, you can extract valuable insights that will serve you well in future endeavors.

Creating an Action Plan

Once you've identified lessons learned, create an action plan to implement these insights. For instance, if you struggled with time management that led to a poor test score, you might set specific goals to improve your study habits. This proactive approach empowers you to take control of your learning and personal growth.

Embracing Future Challenges

Embracing Risk

As you learn to embrace setbacks, it's essential to recognize that taking risks is a vital part of personal development. Whether trying out for a new team, auditioning for a play, or speaking up in class, pushing yourself outside your comfort zone is necessary for growth. The fear of failure can be paralyzing, but embracing the possibility of setbacks can lead to rewarding experiences and accomplishments.

Building a Positive Feedback Loop

As you begin to reframe setbacks and embrace them as learning opportunities, you'll create a positive feedback loop. Each time you successfully navigate a challenge, you'll build confidence, resilience, and the willingness to take on new challenges. This ongoing process contributes to a robust sense of self-efficacy—the belief in your ability to succeed.

Life is an intricate tapestry woven with both triumphs and setbacks. Learning to embrace setbacks as learning opportunities transforms how you experience challenges, promotes resilience, and fosters personal growth. As you navigate the complexities of teenage life, remember that setbacks do not define you; rather, they are moments of learning and growth that shape who you are becoming.

In this journey, practice patience and self-compassion. Recognize that growth takes time, and every setback is a stepping stone toward becoming your best self. By embracing these challenges, you are not just surviving; you are thriving, learning, and evolving into the resilient individual you are meant to be.

Cultivating Gratitude and Positive Affirmations

In the hustle and bustle of teenage life, where challenges abound and pressures mount, it's easy to get caught in a cycle of negativity. This is especially true for those who struggle with anxiety and overthinking. Fortunately, cultivating gratitude and practicing positive affirmations can be transformative tools that help reframe your mindset, reduce stress, and enhance overall well-being. Let's dive deep into how you can integrate these practices into your life and why they are essential for mental health.

Understanding Gratitude

Gratitude is more than just a feeling; it's a practice that involves recognizing and appreciating the positives in your life, no matter how small they may seem. Research has shown that regularly practicing gratitude can lead to numerous mental health benefits, including:

- **Improved Mood**: A simple act of acknowledging what you're thankful for can boost your mood and increase overall happiness. Gratitude shifts your focus from what you lack to what you have, creating a more positive outlook on life.
- **Reduced Anxiety and Depression**: Studies suggest that gratitude can reduce symptoms of anxiety and depression. When you concentrate on positive aspects of your life, it becomes harder to dwell on negative thoughts that can lead to anxiety.
- **Enhanced Resilience**: Practicing gratitude can foster resilience, helping you to bounce back from setbacks and view challenges as opportunities for growth rather than obstacles.
- **Better Relationships**: Expressing gratitude can strengthen your relationships with friends and family. It fosters a sense of connection and appreciation, leading to deeper, more meaningful interactions.

How to Cultivate Gratitude

Cultivating gratitude doesn't have to be complex. Here are several practical strategies to incorporate gratitude into your daily life:

1. **Gratitude Journaling**: Dedicate a few minutes each day to write down three to five things you're grateful for. These can be as simple as enjoying a sunny day, having a supportive friend, or finishing a challenging assignment. The key is to be specific. Instead of writing "I'm grateful for my family," try "I'm grateful for my mom's warm smile and how she always makes me feel loved."
2. **Gratitude Jar**: Create a gratitude jar where you can drop in notes of things you appreciate. At the end of each week or month, read through the notes to remind yourself of the positives in your life. This visual representation of gratitude can be particularly uplifting.
3. **Mindful Appreciation**: Take a few moments each day to mindfully appreciate something around you. It could be the beauty of nature, the taste of your favorite food, or the laughter of friends. Engage your senses and be fully present in the moment.
4. **Express Gratitude to Others**: Make it a habit to thank people in your life. Whether it's sending a text to a friend, writing a letter to a mentor, or simply expressing appreciation to your parents, acknowledging the support and kindness of others reinforces your gratitude practice and strengthens relationships.

5. **Reflect on Challenges**: Sometimes, challenges can lead to growth and new perspectives. Reflect on difficult experiences and identify what you learned or how they helped shape you. This reframing can create a sense of gratitude for the resilience you developed through adversity.

Understanding Positive Affirmations

Positive affirmations are short, powerful statements that help challenge and overcome negative thoughts and beliefs. They reinforce a positive self-image and foster an optimistic mindset. The power of affirmations lies in their ability to reshape your internal dialogue, encouraging you to embrace a more positive view of yourself and your capabilities.

Research supports the effectiveness of affirmations. When you repeat positive affirmations regularly, you can change your thought patterns, reducing anxiety and increasing self-confidence. They serve as a powerful tool to combat self-doubt and fear, particularly in a world where teens often face unrealistic expectations and comparison.

How to Practice Positive Affirmations

Implementing positive affirmations into your daily routine can be straightforward and impactful. Here are some effective strategies:

1. **Identify Your Negative Beliefs**: Start by recognizing negative beliefs or self-talk patterns. These might include thoughts like "I'm not good enough," "I always mess up," or "I'll never fit in." Acknowledging these thoughts is the first step toward change.
2. **Create Your Affirmations**: Transform these negative beliefs into positive statements. For instance, instead of saying, "I'm not good enough," try "I am enough just as I am." Keep your affirmations simple, specific, and in the present tense, as if they are already true.
3. **Make Affirmations Visible**: Write your affirmations down and place them where you can see them daily—on your mirror, your phone, or your bedroom wall. This constant visual reminder will help reinforce positive thinking.
4. **Incorporate Affirmations into Your Routine**: Integrate affirmations into your daily routine. You might say them in the morning while getting ready, during a walk, or as part of your bedtime routine. Repetition helps ingrain these positive messages in your subconscious mind.
5. **Practice with Intent**: When you say your affirmations, do so with intention. Close your eyes, take a deep breath, and visualize what it feels like to embody those statements. Engage with the emotions associated with each affirmation, allowing them to resonate within you.
6. **Combine Gratitude and Affirmations**: You can create a powerful synergy by combining gratitude with affirmations. For instance, while expressing gratitude for a

supportive friend, you might affirm, "I am deserving of love and support." This integration reinforces both practices and enhances their effectiveness.

Overcoming Challenges

While cultivating gratitude and practicing positive affirmations can be incredibly beneficial, you may encounter challenges along the way. Here are a few common obstacles and how to navigate them:

- **Skepticism**: If you feel skeptical about the effectiveness of gratitude or affirmations, start small. Focus on one positive statement or one thing you're grateful for each day. Over time, you may find that your perspective begins to shift.
- **Negative Environment**: Surrounding yourself with negativity can make it hard to maintain a grateful mindset. Seek out supportive friends and environments that encourage positivity. Engage in activities that uplift you and limit exposure to negative influences, including social media.
- **Consistency**: Like any new habit, consistency is key. Set a specific time each day to practice gratitude and affirmations. Consider pairing it with another routine, like brushing your teeth or having breakfast, to help it become a natural part of your day.

Cultivating gratitude and practicing positive affirmations are powerful strategies for overcoming anxiety, managing overthinking, and fostering a positive mindset. These practices not only enhance your mental well-being but also help you build resilience against life's challenges. As you embark on this journey, remember that change takes time. Be patient with yourself, and celebrate even the smallest victories along the way.

By integrating gratitude and positive affirmations into your daily life, you can create a lasting shift in how you perceive yourself and the world around you. The more you practice, the more you will discover the richness of life, the power of your thoughts, and the beauty of who you truly are.

Chapter 9: The Importance of Self-Care and Asking for Help

The Mind-Body Connection: Sleep, Nutrition, and Exercise

As teenagers navigate the complexities of adolescence—school pressures, social dynamics, and the exploration of their identities—self-care often takes a backseat. However, the importance of nurturing our physical, emotional, and mental well-being cannot be overstated. In this chapter, we will explore the intricate relationship between self-care and mental health, emphasizing the critical role that sleep, nutrition, and exercise play in maintaining a healthy mind and body.

Understanding the Mind-Body Connection

To fully appreciate the importance of self-care, we must first understand the mind-body connection. This concept refers to the way our mental and emotional states influence our physical health and vice versa. When we experience stress, anxiety, or sadness, it can manifest physically as fatigue, tension, or even illness. Conversely, our physical health—what we eat, how much we sleep, and how active we are—can significantly impact our mental and emotional well-being.

Research has shown that individuals who practice self-care—those who prioritize adequate sleep, maintain a balanced diet, and engage in regular physical activity—tend to experience lower levels of anxiety and depression. It is essential for teenagers to recognize this connection and understand that by caring for their bodies, they can foster healthier minds.

Sleep: The Foundation of Well-Being

Sleep is one of the most crucial components of self-care. Yet, it is often the first thing to be sacrificed in our busy lives. Teenagers need approximately 8 to 10 hours of sleep per night for optimal functioning. Unfortunately, factors like social obligations, academic pressures, and the allure of technology can lead to poor sleep habits, creating a cycle of exhaustion and overthinking.

The Effects of Sleep Deprivation

Lack of sleep can affect teenagers in numerous ways, including:

- Cognitive Impairment: Sleep deprivation can hinder concentration, memory, and decision-making abilities. For students, this can translate to poor academic performance and increased anxiety about school.

- Emotional Instability: Insufficient sleep is linked to mood swings, irritability, and heightened emotional sensitivity. This instability can strain relationships with peers and family.

- Physical Health Issues: Chronic sleep deprivation is associated with a range of health issues, including obesity, diabetes, and cardiovascular problems. This creates a dangerous feedback loop: poor physical health can lead to anxiety, which further disrupts sleep.

Tips for Better Sleep Hygiene

To combat sleep deprivation, establishing a healthy sleep routine is essential. Here are some practical strategies for improving sleep hygiene:

1. Establish a Sleep Schedule: Going to bed and waking up at the same time every day helps regulate your body's internal clock. Consistency is key.

2. Create a Restful Environment: Your bedroom should be a sanctuary for sleep. Keep the room dark, cool, and quiet. Consider using blackout curtains, earplugs, or white noise machines if needed.

3. Limit Screen Time: The blue light emitted by phones, tablets, and computers can interfere with the production of melatonin, the hormone that regulates sleep. Aim to unplug at least an hour before bedtime.

4. Relax Before Bed: Incorporate calming activities into your evening routine, such as reading, meditation, or gentle stretching. These practices can help signal to your body that it's time to wind down.

5. Watch Your Diet: Avoid heavy meals, caffeine, and sugary snacks close to bedtime. Instead, opt for light snacks that promote sleep, such as bananas or almonds.

Nutrition: Fueling Your Body and Mind

Just as sleep is fundamental to self-care, nutrition plays a pivotal role in our mental health. The food we consume can have profound effects on our mood, energy levels, and overall well-being.

It's essential for teenagers to nourish their bodies with balanced, nutritious foods to support their mental health.

The Impact of Nutrition on Mental Health

Certain nutrients are particularly beneficial for mental health. Here are some key components to consider:

- Omega-3 Fatty Acids: Found in fatty fish (like salmon and mackerel), walnuts, and flaxseeds, omega-3s are known to support brain function and may reduce symptoms of anxiety and depression.

- Complex Carbohydrates: Foods such as whole grains, fruits, and vegetables help stabilize blood sugar levels and provide a steady source of energy. These foods can improve mood and cognitive function.

- Vitamins and Minerals: Nutrients such as B vitamins, magnesium, and zinc play crucial roles in brain health. A deficiency in these vitamins can lead to increased anxiety and depressive symptoms.

- Hydration: Staying hydrated is vital for maintaining optimal cognitive function. Dehydration can lead to fatigue, irritability, and difficulty concentrating. Aim for at least 8 cups of water a day, and more if you're physically active.

Tips for Healthy Eating

Incorporating healthy eating habits into your routine can be simple and enjoyable. Here are some strategies to foster better nutrition:

1. Plan Your Meals: Preparing meals in advance can help you make healthier choices. Consider setting aside time each week to plan and prep nutritious meals and snacks.

2. Eat Mindfully: Pay attention to your hunger cues and eat slowly. This practice not only enhances your enjoyment of food but also helps prevent overeating.

3. Explore New Foods: Experimenting with different fruits, vegetables, and whole grains can make healthy eating exciting. Try to include a variety of colors on your plate for a range of nutrients.

4. Limit Processed Foods: While it can be tempting to reach for quick and convenient snacks, try to limit processed foods high in sugars and unhealthy fats. Instead, opt for whole foods that nourish your body.

Exercise: Moving for Mental Clarity

Physical activity is another vital aspect of self-care that significantly impacts mental health. Exercise releases endorphins, the body's natural mood lifters, and can provide a sense of accomplishment and purpose. Regular physical activity helps to reduce anxiety, improve mood, and promote better sleep.

The Benefits of Exercise

Incorporating exercise into your routine can offer numerous mental health benefits, including:

- Reduced Symptoms of Anxiety and Depression: Studies show that regular physical activity can be as effective as medication for some individuals dealing with mild to moderate anxiety and depression.

- Improved Self-Esteem: Achieving fitness goals, no matter how small, can enhance self-confidence and promote a positive self-image.

- Stress Relief: Exercise can serve as a powerful outlet for stress. It provides a break from negative thoughts and helps clear your mind.

- Enhanced Cognitive Function: Physical activity increases blood flow to the brain, which can improve focus, creativity, and overall cognitive function.

Tips for Staying Active

Finding ways to incorporate physical activity into your daily routine doesn't have to be a chore. Here are some strategies to make exercise enjoyable:

1. Choose Activities You Enjoy: Whether it's dancing, hiking, swimming, or playing a sport, engaging in activities you love makes exercise feel less like a duty and more like a pleasure.

2. Start Small: If you're new to exercise, start with short sessions of 10-15 minutes and gradually increase the duration and intensity. Consistency is more important than intensity.

3. Get Moving with Friends: Exercising with friends can make it more enjoyable and provide accountability. Consider joining a sports team, a dance class, or a local running group.

4. Incorporate Movement into Your Day: Look for opportunities to be active throughout your day. Take the stairs instead of the elevator, go for a walk during lunch, or do a quick workout at home.

Asking for Help: A Crucial Component of Self-Care

While sleep, nutrition, and exercise are vital to self-care, it is equally important to recognize when we need help and to ask for it. Many teens feel pressure to appear strong and independent, which can lead to isolating feelings and overwhelm. However, seeking support is a sign of strength, not weakness.

The Importance of Seeking Support

Asking for help can take many forms. Whether it's confiding in a friend, reaching out to a family member, or speaking with a mental health professional, support can provide:

- A Different Perspective: Talking through your feelings can help you gain clarity and insight. Others may offer solutions or coping strategies you hadn't considered.

- Emotional Validation: Sometimes, just knowing that someone else understands what you're going through can be incredibly comforting. It reminds you that you're not alone.

- Practical Support: Friends and family can provide tangible support, such as helping you manage your time, encouraging healthy habits, or simply being there to listen.

Overcoming Barriers to Seeking Help

Despite the benefits of seeking support, many teens hesitate to reach out. Common barriers include fear of judgment, feelings of shame, or the belief that they should be able to handle everything on their own. To overcome these barriers:

1. Normalize Help-Seeking: Understand that everyone needs help at times. Seeking support is a healthy part of life, and it's okay to reach out when you're feeling overwhelmed.

2. Communicate Your Needs: Be open about what you're experiencing. You don't have to share everything at once—start with what feels comfortable and gradually open up more as you feel ready.

3. Consider Professional Support: If you find that your anxiety or stress is overwhelming, seeking the guidance of a therapist can be beneficial. Mental health professionals can provide you with tailored strategies to cope effectively.

4. Build a Support Network: Cultivating relationships with friends, family, and mentors can create a safety net. Surround yourself with individuals who uplift and support you.

Creating a Self-Care Routine

In today's fast-paced world, the pressures on teenagers can feel overwhelming. From schoolwork and extracurricular activities to social dynamics and the pervasive influence of social media, it's no wonder that many young adults experience anxiety, stress, and feelings of being overwhelmed. A self-care routine can be a powerful tool for managing these pressures and fostering overall well-being. This guide will explore the importance of self-care, provide detailed steps for creating a personalized routine, and offer tips on how to stick with it.

Understanding Self-Care

What is Self-Care?
Self-care refers to the practices and activities we engage in to promote our physical, mental, and emotional health. It's about taking intentional actions that prioritize your well-being. For teens, self-care can encompass a wide range of activities, from physical exercise to creative outlets, mindfulness practices, and social connections.

Why is Self-Care Important?

1. **Reduces Stress and Anxiety:** Engaging in self-care activities can help alleviate feelings of stress and anxiety. When you take time for yourself, it allows your body and mind to recharge and reset.
2. **Enhances Mood and Emotional Well-Being:** Regular self-care practices can improve your mood, boost self-esteem, and contribute to a more positive outlook on life.
3. **Promotes Better Physical Health:** Taking care of your body through proper nutrition, exercise, and rest can lead to improved physical health, reducing the likelihood of illness and fatigue.
4. **Improves Resilience:** A well-rounded self-care routine can enhance your ability to cope with life's challenges, making you more resilient in the face of adversity.

Steps to Create Your Self-Care Routine

Step 1: Reflect on Your Needs

Begin by identifying what areas of your life need the most attention. Consider the following questions:

- What stresses you out the most?
- Are there particular situations or people that drain your energy?
- What activities make you feel rejuvenated and happy?
- Do you feel physically tired or mentally exhausted?

Taking the time to reflect on these questions will help you understand your unique needs and preferences.

Step 2: Explore Different Self-Care Activities

Self-care can take many forms. Here are some categories to consider when exploring activities:

1. **Physical Self-Care:**
   - **Exercise:** Engage in activities like dancing, swimming, jogging, or yoga. Aim for at least 30 minutes of physical activity most days of the week.
   - **Nutrition:** Eat balanced meals that nourish your body. Try to incorporate fruits, vegetables, whole grains, and lean proteins into your diet.
   - **Sleep:** Aim for 7-9 hours of quality sleep each night. Create a calming bedtime routine to help you unwind.
2. **Emotional Self-Care:**
   - **Journaling:** Write about your thoughts and feelings. This practice can help you process emotions and gain clarity.
   - **Mindfulness and Meditation:** Try mindfulness exercises or guided meditations to ground yourself in the present moment.
   - **Expressing Gratitude:** Maintain a gratitude journal where you list things you're thankful for each day. This can shift your perspective towards positivity.
3. **Social Self-Care:**
   - **Spend Time with Loved Ones:** Schedule regular hangouts with friends or family members who uplift you.
   - **Join Clubs or Groups:** Participate in extracurricular activities that interest you, such as art clubs, sports teams, or volunteer groups.
   - **Communicate Your Needs:** Don't hesitate to share your feelings with trusted friends or adults. Open communication can deepen relationships and provide support.
4. **Creative Self-Care:**
   - **Art and Crafting:** Explore your creativity through painting, drawing, or crafting.
   - **Music:** Listen to music that inspires you or play an instrument. Music can be a powerful emotional outlet.

- ○ **Writing:** Write stories, poems, or blogs to express your thoughts and experiences.
5. **Spiritual Self-Care:**
   - ○ **Nature Walks:** Spend time in nature to connect with the world around you.
   - ○ **Meditation or Prayer:** If you have a spiritual practice, dedicate time to connect with your beliefs.
   - ○ **Mindfulness:** Practice being present, focusing on your breath, or engaging in mindful observation of your surroundings.

Step 3: Schedule Your Self-Care Activities

Once you've identified activities that resonate with you, it's time to incorporate them into your daily life. Consider the following:

- **Create a Self-Care Calendar:** Use a planner or digital calendar to schedule self-care activities throughout your week. Treat these appointments as non-negotiable.
- **Start Small:** If you're new to self-care, start with small, manageable activities. Gradually increase the time and frequency as you become more comfortable.
- **Be Flexible:** Life can be unpredictable, so be open to adjusting your routine as needed. The goal is to prioritize self-care, not add more stress.

Step 4: Evaluate and Adjust Your Routine

Your self-care routine is not set in stone. Periodically evaluate how you're feeling and whether your activities are serving your needs. Ask yourself:

- Are you feeling more balanced and less stressed?
- Are there activities that you're not enjoying?
- Do you need to try something new to keep your routine fresh?

Make adjustments based on your reflections, and don't be afraid to explore new activities as your interests and needs evolve.

Tips for Sticking to Your Self-Care Routine

1. **Set Reminders:** Use alarms or apps to remind you of your self-care activities. This can help you stay committed, especially during busy weeks.
2. **Accountability Partners:** Share your self-care goals with a friend or family member who can encourage you and hold you accountable.
3. **Celebrate Your Progress:** Acknowledge and celebrate your efforts, no matter how small. Treat yourself when you reach milestones or successfully integrate self-care into your routine.
4. **Be Kind to Yourself:** If you miss a self-care session or feel overwhelmed, avoid self-criticism. Acknowledge that it's okay to have off days and recommit to your routine when you're ready.

5. **Keep It Enjoyable:** Choose activities that genuinely bring you joy and relaxation. Self-care should never feel like a chore.

Creating a self-care routine is a vital step towards managing stress and promoting overall well-being. By reflecting on your needs, exploring various activities, and committing to a consistent routine, you can cultivate a healthy relationship with yourself. Remember that self-care is a journey, not a destination. Embrace the process, and allow yourself the grace to grow and adapt along the way. Ultimately, prioritizing your well-being will empower you to face life's challenges with resilience, confidence, and clarity.

Talking It Out: Building a Support System

Overthinking, anxiety, and stress can be incredibly isolating. When you're caught in a whirlwind of anxious thoughts, it's easy to believe that no one understands you or that you need to carry the weight of your worries alone. But here's the truth: you don't have to. In fact, trying to go it alone often makes things worse. One of the most effective ways to break free from the cycle of overthinking and anxiety is by talking it out and building a strong support system.

Let's dive deep into why talking about your struggles matters, how it can ease the burden of overthinking, and how to build a network of support that helps you feel seen, understood, and supported.

Why Talking It Out Matters

When your mind is stuck in overdrive—replaying events, imagining worst-case scenarios, or feeling overwhelmed by everything on your plate—those thoughts can feel like they are snowballing inside your head. Talking out loud, whether it's to a friend, family member, or therapist, can give you a sense of relief. Why? Because when you talk, you're no longer carrying all of that emotional and mental weight alone.

Sharing your thoughts often gives you perspective. When you're trapped in a cycle of overthinking, everything feels larger and more intense than it really is. By expressing your feelings out loud, you start to make sense of them. It's as if your thoughts transform from something hazy and confusing into something more concrete and manageable. When you articulate what's troubling you, your brain can often see the situation more clearly, allowing you to sort through the chaos.

Additionally, talking it out activates parts of the brain that help with emotional regulation. Studies in neuroscience show that verbalizing your feelings engages the prefrontal cortex, which is involved in decision-making and emotional control. Essentially, when you talk about your stressors, you're giving your brain a chance to process emotions rather than being overwhelmed by them.

How Overthinking Thrives in Silence

Silence can be fertile ground for overthinking. When you keep your thoughts to yourself, they often feel more powerful and persistent. Overthinking thrives when there's no external input to challenge it. The more you stay quiet, the more your thoughts have room to spiral, growing more intense and disconnected from reality.

For example, let's say you're anxious about a presentation at school. Without talking to someone about your fears, your mind might spin wild stories about all the things that could go wrong—tripping on stage, forgetting your words, everyone judging you. But if you open up to a trusted friend or teacher about your worries, they can provide reassurance or share their own experiences, which helps you see that your fears are exaggerated.

Isolation also makes it easier for negative thought patterns to set in. If you don't share your anxieties, you may start to believe that no one else goes through what you're experiencing, or worse, that people might think less of you if they knew. This shame can trap you in a cycle of self-criticism and perfectionism, where you feel like you need to solve everything on your own. But here's the thing: vulnerability is not weakness. Talking about your struggles shows strength and the desire to grow.

Who Can Be Part of Your Support System?

A support system is like a safety net—you want it to be strong, flexible, and reliable. But it doesn't have to be huge. A few key people who genuinely care about your well-being can make all the difference. So, who can you turn to when you're feeling overwhelmed?

1. **Friends**
   Your friends are often the people who know you best. They've seen you at your worst and your best, and they're more likely to understand the context behind your worries. Plus, because they're in similar life stages, they might relate to your struggles in ways others can't. Whether it's venting over text, hanging out in person, or having a deep conversation late at night, friends can offer comfort and perspective. Sometimes, just knowing someone is there can take the edge off your anxiety.

2. **Family**
   While relationships with family members can sometimes be complicated, they can also offer a strong foundation of support. Whether it's a parent, sibling, or extended family member, talking to someone in your family can remind you that you're not facing your challenges alone. Family members, especially those who've known you all your life, can

provide unique insights into patterns you may not even be aware of and help you recognize the strength you've shown in the past.

3. **Teachers or Coaches**

   Sometimes, an adult outside of your immediate family, like a teacher, counselor, or coach, can offer valuable advice and support. They may have been through similar struggles themselves, or they may have helped other young people navigate anxiety and stress. Because they're a little removed from your daily life, they might be able to offer a fresh perspective or practical advice that you hadn't considered.

4. **Therapists or Counselors**

   Speaking with a mental health professional can be one of the most powerful tools in managing anxiety and overthinking. Unlike friends or family, therapists are trained to listen in a way that helps you explore your thoughts and feelings more deeply. They can help you identify patterns in your thinking and behaviors, teach you coping strategies, and provide a non-judgmental space for you to express yourself. Therapy doesn't mean there's something "wrong" with you—it's a space for growth, healing, and self-discovery.

5. **Online Communities**

   If you don't feel comfortable talking to people in your immediate environment, consider joining online support groups. There are many communities dedicated to mental health, overthinking, and anxiety. Sometimes, the anonymity of an online space can make it easier to open up, and you can connect with others who are going through similar challenges. While it's important to be cautious online, finding a supportive digital space can help you feel less alone.

How to Start the Conversation

Opening up about your feelings isn't always easy. It can feel vulnerable, especially if you're not used to sharing your emotions. But remember, you don't have to dive into a deep conversation right away. Start small. Here are a few ways you can approach talking it out:

- **"I've been feeling really overwhelmed lately, and I could use someone to talk to. Do you have time?"**

  This shows that you're ready to share but gives the other person space to be present with you when they're available.

- **"I've been stuck in my head a lot, and it's stressing me out. I think talking about it might help."**

  This makes it clear that you're seeking help with overthinking, and you're open to feedback or simply being listened to.

- **"I'm not looking for solutions right now—I just need someone to listen. Could you do that?"**

  Sometimes, people might jump straight into problem-solving mode when you really just want to be heard. Letting them know what you need upfront can make the conversation feel more supportive.

Once you open up, you might be surprised by how understanding people can be. Most people have experienced anxiety or stress at some point in their lives, and sharing your experiences often invites others to share their own. Talking about mental health can help break down the stigma, showing that it's normal to struggle and even more normal to ask for help.

Sustaining Your Support System

Building a support system isn't a one-time effort—it's an ongoing process. Relationships require nurturing. To keep your support system strong, remember to:

- **Check in regularly** with the people who support you. Even when you're feeling okay, maintaining those connections ensures that when you do need help, the relationship is already strong.
- **Reciprocate** the support. Be there for others when they're struggling, too. This doesn't mean you have to take on their problems, but showing empathy and being a good listener can strengthen the bond you have with your support system.
- **Communicate your needs clearly.** If you're going through a particularly rough patch, it's okay to let others know what you need, whether it's advice, a distraction, or just a comforting presence.
- **Don't hesitate to reach out to professionals** when your support system can't meet your needs. There's no shame in seeking professional help, and therapists can provide tools and guidance that friends or family might not be equipped to offer.

Talking it out and building a support system isn't just about venting—it's about sharing your burden and gaining insight from others. It's a crucial part of managing overthinking and anxiety. When you open up and allow yourself to be vulnerable, you'll find that you're not alone in your struggles. People want to help. All you have to do is take that first step.

Conclusion

As we come to the end of this journey, I want to remind you of something important: overcoming overthinking is not about becoming perfect or never feeling anxious again. It's about learning how to manage your mind, even when things feel overwhelming. It's about recognizing that your thoughts don't control you—you control them.

Think back to where we started. You might have felt like you were trapped in your own mind, unable to escape the endless cycle of worries and "what-ifs." But now, you've equipped yourself with tools to break free from that cycle. Through mindfulness, you've learned how to pause, take a breath, and ground yourself in the present moment. You've discovered that your mind is powerful, but with the right skills, you can guide it rather than let it run wild.

You might still have days where overthinking creeps back in. That's okay. The process of managing your thoughts, like any skill, takes time and practice. But each time you use what you've learned—whether it's a breathing exercise, a grounding technique, or simply recognizing when you're caught in a loop—you're taking a step forward. Every small victory matters.

The beauty of mindfulness is that it's always available to you, no matter where you are or what's going on in your life. You don't need any special tools or a quiet space. You just need the awareness to recognize when your mind is getting carried away, and the willingness to bring it back. And the more you practice, the more natural it will become.

As you move forward, I encourage you to continue exploring what works best for you. Maybe it's daily meditation, or maybe it's just taking a mindful moment when you feel stress creeping in. Whatever it is, trust that you have what it takes to manage your thoughts and reduce the anxiety that comes with overthinking.

Remember, you are not defined by your anxious thoughts. You are strong, capable, and resilient. You've already taken the hardest step by acknowledging that overthinking doesn't have to control your life. Now, you have the tools to create a sense of calm, even in the middle of chaos.

This is just the beginning of your journey. Life will throw challenges your way, but with the skills you've developed, you'll face them with clarity and confidence. You can now approach your thoughts with curiosity rather than fear, and you have the power to respond to life's difficulties in a way that protects your peace of mind.

Overcoming overthinking is not a destination; it's a path that you'll walk every day. But the good news is, you're no longer walking it alone. You have your mindfulness skills, your self-awareness, and your inner strength to guide you.

So, take a deep breath. Trust yourself. And step forward with confidence, knowing that you have everything you need to manage anxiety, stress, and whatever challenges may come. You've already started the journey toward a clearer, calmer mind—and you're well on your way to living a life where overthinking no longer holds you back.

The path ahead is yours to walk, and you're ready.

Bonus

Guided Audio Meditations and Video

SCAN TO GET ACCESS
TO YOUR BONUS

INDEX